"Stretching"
Exercises for
Qualitative
Researchers

"Stretching" Exercises for Qualitative Researchers

Valerie J. Janesick

SAGE Publications
International Educational and Professional Publisher
Thousand Oaks   London   New Delhi

For information:

SAGE Publications, Inc.
2455 Teller Road
Thousand Oaks, California 91320
E-mail: order@sagepub.com

SAGE Publications Ltd.
6 Bonhill Street
London EC2A 4PU
United Kingdom

SAGE Publications India Pvt. Ltd.
M-32 Market
Greater Kailash I
New Delhi 110 048 India

Printed in the United States of America

Library of Congress Cataloging-in-Publication Data

Janesick, Valerie J.
  "Stretching" exercises for qualitative researchers / by Valerie J. Janesick.
    p. cm.
  Includes bibliographical references and index.
  ISBN 0-7619-0255-4 (cloth : acid-free paper). —ISBN 0-7619-0256-2
  (pbk.: acid-free paper)
    1. Social sciences—Research—Methodology. 2. Observation
  (Scientific method) 3. Qualitative reasoning. I. Title.
    H62.J346 1998
    330'.72—dc21   97-33905

This book is printed on acid-free paper.

98 99 00 01 02 03 10 9 8 7 6 5 4 3 2 1

Acquiring Editor:	Peter Labella
Editorial Assistant:	Corinne Pierce
Production Editor:	Sherrise M. Purdum
Production Assistant:	Lynn Miyata
Typesetter/Designer:	Marion Warren
Indexer:	Molly Hall
Cover Designer:	Candice Harman
Print Buyer:	Anna Chin

Contents ■

Foreword   xi

Acknowledgments   xv

■ **Part 1: Introduction**   **1**

Background   1
Some Notes on Theory   5
Hindsight   8
How to Use This Book   9
The Audience for This Book   10

■ **Part 2: Observation Exercises**   **13**

■ *Exercise 1:*
  Observing a Still Life Scene   14
Constructing a Reflective Portfolio   17
■ *Exercise 2:*
  Physical Description of This Setting   18

■ *Exercise 3:*
Observation in the Home or Workplace   19

■ *Exercise 4:*
Description of a Familiar Person   20

■ *Exercise 5:*
Observing a Stranger   21

■ *Exercise 6:*
Observing an Animal at Home,
the Zoo, or a Pet Shop   22

■ *Exercise 7:*
Nonparticipant Observation Assignment   23

Next Steps   25

Summary of Part 2: The Observation Cycle   25

Pitfalls and Guidelines   27

■ **Part 3: The Interview Cycle**   **29**

Two People Talking, Communication,
   and Constructing Meaning   30

Types of Interview Questions   30

Preparing Questions   31

■ *Exercise 1:*
Interviewing Someone You Know   32

■ *Exercise 2:*
Interviewing a Stranger   33

■ *Exercise 3:*
Phone Interviews   33

About Focus Groups   34

■ *Exercise 4:*
The Focus Group Interview   39

■ *Exercise 5:*
Analyzing Interview Data   41

Summary and Pitfalls   42

■ **Part 4: Personal Development and the
Role of the Researcher Cycle
Selected Exercises** **45**

■ *Exercise 1:*
Writing Your Name 46

■ *Exercise 2:*
Photography Exercise 48

■ *Exercise 3:*
Building a Collage: My Role as a Researcher 49

■ *Exercise 4:*
Constructing a YaYa Box 50

■ *Exercise 5:*
*Journal Dialogue with Persons, Works,
the Body, Society, and Major Life Events* 53

■ *Exercise 6:*
Haiku and the Role of the Researcher 54

■ *Exercise 7:*
Framed Photograph Exercise 55

Summary of Part 4: Personal Development and
the Role of the Researcher 56

■ **Part 5: The Analysis Cycle:
Intuition, Ethics, and Other Issues** **59**

The Qualitative Researcher as Historian 60

The Qualitative Researcher as User of
All Senses Including the Intuitive Sense 61

The Qualitative Researcher and the O. Henry Virus 63

Checkpoints for Data Analysis, Reporting,
and Interpretation 64

Ethics and the Qualitative Researcher 65

True Stories: Sample Ethical Dilemmas 65

Rules of Thumb for Qualitative Researchers 67

Attributes of the Qualitative Researcher 69

Summary 72

Appendix A:
Interview Protocol: Perspectives on Deafness 75

Appendix B:
Nonparticipant Observation—Fieldnotes
  Kim Zier (excerpts) 76

Appendix C:
Sample Floor Plan 77

Appendix D:
Sample Journal Entry
  A Journal of My Research Process
    Beth Easter (selected excerpts) 78

Appendix E:
Student Journal in the Field
  Peter Gitau 80

Appendix F:
Self-Evaluation From a Former Student
  David Smith 82

Appendix G:
Summative Evaluation Sample—Self-Report
  The Power of Transformative Agency
    Patricia Williams Boyd 83

Appendix H:
Qualitative Research Methods—A Sample Syllabus
  Instructor: Valerie J. Janesick 84

  Class Calendar 89

Appendix I:
Sample In-Class Handouts
  Terms Used to Identify Qualitative Work
  (these are not meant to be all inclusive) 90

Appendix J:
Characteristics of Qualitative Design 91

Appendix K:
Questions Suited to Qualitative Inquiry   92

Appendix L:
Sample Miniprojects From Various Classes   93

Appendix M:
Sample Consent Forms   94
 Exhibit A   94
 Exhibit B   94

Appendix N:
Suggested Sections for the Qualitative Research Proposal   95
 Chapter 1: Introduction and Purpose   95
 Chapter 2: Review of Related Literature   96
 Chapter 3: Methods Used in This Study   96

Appendix O:
Samples of Dissertation Proposals
 With Focus on Methodology   99
 Sample 1: Dennis Dolan
  An Outline of a Completed Dissertation Proposal
  Using Interviews, Documents, and Observations   99
 Sample 2: Marilyn Kaff
  A Proposal That Uses Focus Groups,
  Interviews, Artifacts, and Observations   101
 Sample 3: Patricia Williams Boyd
  Example of a Dissertation Proposal Using
  Interviews, Observations, Photography,
  and Documents   111

Appendix P:
Guidelines for Mini Project   128
 Guidelines for the Final Report of Your Mini Project   128

Index   131

About the Author   135

Foreword ■

One of the important contributions of tenure is to enable pro-
fessors to write the kind of book that Valerie Janesick has
written. It is a book whose dominant metaphors are artistic and
whose focus is practical. The arts have seldom enjoyed a position
of respect in the social sciences; those of us working in the social
sciences adore different gods: the literal more than the metaphori-
cal, the precise more than the ambiguous, the predictable more
than the uncertain. And, as for practicality, the practical person
tends also to live an uncomfortable life in the theoretical universe
that university faculty aspire to create. Valerie Janesick has given
us a practical book that is artistically inspired. That is no mean
accomplishment.

She recognizes quite clearly that the two major functions that
are addressed in *"Stretching" Exercises for Qualitative Researchers*,
observing and interviewing, are both key processes for learning.
Observing is all too often taken for granted. At one level, all of us
observe, and we require no instruction to do so. But what Valerie
Janesick means by observing, at least as implied in her writing, is
not merely observing, but *seeing* what has been observed. In a
prosaic way, *observing* is a task term. It is something that you do.
Seeing, which is the reward of effective observation, is an achievement term. It is something that you secure. Learning to see what

is observed is at the very core of qualitative research. But even here, the kind of observing that leads to seeing has to be supplemented by another process. The best term I know is *reading*. By reading, I mean making sense, interpreting, giving significance to what has been seen through observation. Qualitative researchers need to do all three. They need to observe, to see, and to read the seen.

Learning to see what you observe is not easy. There are so many factors that interfere with its achievement, not the least of which is routine. We all require routines, those habits of mind that allow us to negotiate the world with the least amount of effort. There is, after all, an important benefit from economizing energy. At the same time, the very comforts and patterns and habits and routines that make such negotiation possible lead most of us to lead semi-lived lives. The familiar not only breeds contempt, it breeds darkness as well. We become accustomed to *not* seeing. And, of course, among the great contributions of the arts and the sciences is their capacity to awaken us from our slumbers, to provide a frame through which we can see the world more clearly or from a new angle. They cultivate surprise.

It is appropriate that the arts have functioned as a core metaphor for Valerie Janesick's work. To observe in a way that allows us to see, we need to free ourselves from old habits. As I said, it's not an easy task, but it is a critical one. Without it, our observations are likely to be pedestrian, and with pedestrian observations, we are unlikely to get much in the way of an interesting reading.

Interviewing, of course, is a mainline toward getting into the lives of people so that our understanding of the nature of their experience is secured. In a sense, interviewing in the context of qualitative research has clinical features to it, and the satisfaction that interviewees often experience when being interviewed by a skilled interviewer is a desire to have the interviewer return. Let's face it, there aren't all that many people around who pay serious attention to what we have to say. When interviewers do, they acknowledge the importance of the individual and his or her life by making the time to pay serious attention.

Interviews, at their best, are like conversations. Conversations are dialectic, organic, and often filled with surprises. And so too should interviews be. Valerie Janesick recognizes the dynamic and uncertain character of the often wandering but interesting course of a good interview. Her book acknowledges it and provides for its occurrence.

What is especially interesting to me in *"Stretching" Exercises for Qualitative Researchers* is her tacit recognition that experience is the medium of education, for what she has done is not simply to talk theoretically about the importance of observation and interviewing, but to provide those exercises that, in the end, generate the kind of experience that will enable students to become more astute observers and interviewers. The exercises are interesting, often challenging, and are likely to be highly informative to those who use them. As I said, tenure is a wonderful thing. It helps make books like this possible.

There is one other aspect of Valerie Janesick's work that I can't help but comment on and that has to do with matters of clarity. In methodological circles, there is often a tendency to become both arcane and obscure in one's language; it is a mark of "scholarship." Valerie Janesick has given us a practical book, rooted productively in the arts, that is clear as a bell. It exemplifies in form and in style what it advocates. That too is often much too much of a novelty in academic writing. All of us need to stretch. *"Stretching" Exercises for Qualitative Researchers* will help us do just that.

Elliot W. Eisner
Stanford, California
May 1, 1997

Acknowledgments ■

I wish to express my deepest gratitude to all those who helped me complete this project in one way or another. First and foremost, to my students I must say thanks for testing me, questioning me, encouraging me, and supporting me with great enthusiasm and affection. To colleagues, friends, reviewers, and critics I am most grateful. Those former students of mine who contributed to the text with samples of their work in progress are generous, and I thank them for their graciousness. They are Judith Gouwens, Dennis Dolan, Ahmed Zafir, Beth Easter, Chin-kuei Cheng, Patricia W. Boyd, Marilyn Kaff, Kim Zier, Peter Gitau, and David Smith.

Finally, thanks to Mitch Allen, who encouraged me to go ahead with this project when we were conversing about it years ago. Most of all, thanks to Peter Labella, a superb editor, and all at Sage who made this process reflective, challenging, and caring. I am indebted.

PART 1

Introduction ■

Research is formalized curiosity. It is poking and prying with purpose.

Zora Neale Hurston

■ Background

This text began in the classroom. As a teacher of graduate students for nearly 20 years now in this area of qualitative methods, I have been fortunate to have been inspired and tested by my doctoral students in Albany, New York, Washington, D.C., Lawrence, Kansas, and now in Miami and Fort Lauderdale. No matter what the geographical setting, the questions they have raised remain nearly the same:

1. How can I become a better qualitative researcher?
2. How can I improve observation skills?
3. How can I improve interview skills?

Realizing that these questions have no easy answers, and realizing there is no one way to respond to these questions, I am using the concept of "stretching exercises" to frame this text, as a response to my students. I have written elsewhere (Janesick, 1994) using dance as a metaphor for qualitative research design, and I would like to extend that metaphor by using the concept of stretching. Stretching implies that you are moving from a static point to

1

an active one. It means you are going beyond the point at which you now stand. Just as the dancer must stretch to begin what eventually becomes the dance, the qualitative researcher may stretch by using these exercises to become better at observation and interview skills, in what eventually solidifies as the research project. These are meant as a starting point, not a slavish set of prescriptions.

As a starting point, I see these exercises as part of shaping the prospective researcher as a disciplined inquirer. *Disciplined inquiry*, a term borrowed from John Dewey, assumes that we begin where we are now and, in a systematic way, proceed together to experience what it might mean to inquire. In this case, practice exercises are used to help in identifying a disciplined inquiry approach. To use ballet as an example, the ballet dancer in training takes a beginning series of classes, intermediate classes, and various levels of advanced classes before going to performance on point. There is no way an individual can skip from beginning to advanced stages in ballet, or in modern dance for that matter. In fact, the modern dance student is often required to study ballet at the advanced level in order to have a stronger ability to do modern dance. Granted once in a blue moon, a dancer like Nureyev comes along. Yet, most of us do not have the gift of a Rudolf Nureyev. One has to develop skill and train the body incrementally. Likewise, the qualitative researcher has to train the mind, and the eye, and the soul, together. By doing these exercises, we allow for an interchange of ideas and practice, self reflection, and overall evaluation of one's own progress through each of the cycles described in this text: (a) The Observation Cycle; (b) The Interview Cycle; (c) The Role of the Researcher Cycle; and (d) The Analysis Cycle, which includes ethics, intuition, and interpretation of data. By assuming a posture of disciplined inquiry, the prospective qualitative researcher is an active agent. This is not about memorizing a formula. This is about constructing a critical space for serious observation and interview skills development. By actually constructing this space, the prospective qualitative researcher automatically begins a labor-intensive and challenging journey, much like the journey of the dancer from first dance class to performance. This journey also involves understanding oneself as the researcher. Consequently, there are some exercises here that may also provide a way to work on the role of the researcher by knowing oneself better. This can be helpful only when engaged full-time with participants in the field. Participants will trust you, the researcher, if you trust yourself.

I have found that learners respond to being actively involved in these practice exercises for a number of reasons. They have told me that these exercises strengthened their confidence, imagination, and ability to cope with field emergencies. (See Appendixes F and G for self-evaluation samples.) In addition, students appreciate the fact that all these exercises are understandable, for the language used to describe them is ordinary language. I have always found students more responsive and enthusiastic when ordinary language is used to include them in the active engagement of qualitative research. They are more excited about theory, practice, and praxis when they are not excluded from the conversation. The reader of this text will see that the exercises are described in *ordinary language*, following in the tradition of bell hooks (1994), who pointed out that any theory that cannot be used in everyday conversation cannot be used to educate. In addition, the actual experience and practice of these exercises in observation and interview activities often help to allay fears and misconceptions about conducting qualitative research projects. Two of the most common misconceptions stated in classes or workshops are: (a) Doing qualitative research looks easy, and (b) Most people can do interviews and observations with little or no practice. In a sense, this text is a response to these two viewpoints. I see these exercises as an opportunity to continue the conversation with individuals who want to take the plunge, to go over the cliff so to speak, and learn something about qualitative research methods. Although I have used these exercises with doctoral students in education and human services, there is the possibility that beginning researchers at the master's degree level may also find these exercises useful, not only in education and human services, but in other disciplines as well.

I engage learners in these exercises over a period of 16 weeks, the artificial constraint of the given semester time line. In the best of all possible worlds, I would prefer a year or more, perhaps three semesters, of work time. I try to divide the course over the 16 weeks into four major cycles:

1. The cycle of observations
2. The cycle of interviews
3. The role of the researcher cycle
4. The analysis cycle

Learners simultaneously design, conceptualize, and conduct a ministudy. Within the study, the learner must conduct interviews and observations. In the first third of the class, learners practice exercises in and out of class focusing on observation and the role of the researcher. The next third of class is spent on interviewing exercises and practice in ongoing analysis. The final third of the class is devoted to final analysis of data and ethical issues. In the best of all worlds, the observation exercises and role of the researcher exercises are practiced for about 5 or 6 weeks, at which point the learners are asked to develop a plan in writing for their ministudy. Then, as they go into the field, they simultaneously work on the interview exercises and role of the researcher exercises for the remainder of the semester, all the while reading selected books and articles in the area. Although this series of exercises grew out of my work with students and workshop members, surely there are others who may be interested in this book. Likewise, the reader of this text can be immersed in these exercises at any pace the individual may choose. Basically, this is an attempt to begin a conversation with individuals who, up to now, may not have had the time, energy, or interest in practicing qualitative techniques but are now ready to jump into the studio of the social world and stretch.

I must digress here to point out that dance as an art form is one of the most rigorous and demanding of the arts. For one thing, physical tone and health are extremely critical to the survival of the dancer. The hours of working out are not only physical, for the physical and mental connection engages the dance artist totally. The dancer's life is a short one in terms of performance, due to dependence on a superbly functioning instrument, the body. I mention all this to punctuate the fact that the discipline and desire of the dancer are persistent and indomitable, much like those of the qualitative researcher. As a professor of qualitative research methods and as a former choreographer and dancer, I see the role of the researcher as one characterized by discipline, persistence, and desire to communicate the findings so as to reflect the social setting and its members, much as the dancer reflects the dance. Likewise, qualitative research methods are related to dance in another way, because the body is the instrument of dance and the researcher is the research instrument in qualitative work.

■ Some Notes on Theory

As the reader is most likely aware, in qualitative work, theory is used at every step of the research process. Theoretical frames influence the questions we ask, the design of the study, the implementation of the study, and the way we interpret data. In addition, qualitative researchers develop theoretical models of what occurred in a study in order to explain their findings. In this approach, theory is grounded in the data (see Glaser & Strauss, 1967, on grounded theory). Qualitative researchers have an obligation to fully describe their theoretical postures at all stages of the research process, as the choreographer fully describes and explains each component of a dance plan.

Speaking for myself, I have had many influences throughout my career, but the most notable influences from my own experience as a teacher include the work of John Dewey on education and art as experience, aesthetics and the work of Elliot Eisner, critical pedagogy and cultural studies and the work of Henry A. Giroux, feminist theory and the work of Jane Flax and bell hooks, and postmodern sociology and the work of Norman Denzin. I call myself a critical, postmodern, interpretive interactionist with a feminist artistry. In addition, the works of Paulo Freire and Myles Horton have influenced my thinking. Horton's idea that we have our own solutions within us fits perfectly with interpretive work. Likewise, Freire's education for freedom is identical to Merce Cunningham's philosophy of dance. My own qualitative research projects have been guided by the theoretical frames of symbolic interactionism and critical pedagogy. This does not mean that other frameworks are incompatible or unuseful. I have great affinity for phenomenology as described by Max Van Manen: for example, the work of Valerie Yow on oral history, and the work being done in medicine by Ben Crabtree, Tony Kuzel, William Miller, Richard Addison, and Valerie Gilchrist. (See Supplemental Readings at the end of this chapter.)

A great deal of the debate over qualitative methods has to do with the issue of theory and its place in the research project. I would characterize this as a struggle between those arguing for the *pedagogy of the answer* versus the *pedagogy of the question* (Bruss & Macedo, 1985). Many feel there is definitive knowledge about how to proceed in research substantively, theoretically, and procedurally. Others see research as a way to pursue moral, ethical, and political questions. I ask learners to think about the pedagogy of the question when it comes to qualitative work. It forces a rethinking of the world in a critical frame:

> The pedagogy of the question requires that learners distance themselves from their bureaucratized daily existence, while they become more aware through reflection of the mythical facts which enslave them. Unlike the pedagogy of the answer, which reduces learners to mere receptacles for prepackaged knowledge, the pedagogy of the question gives learners, the "language of possibility" to challenge the very constraints which relegate them to mere objects. (Bruss & Macedo, 1985, p. 8)

What this means for the purposes of this text and studying qualitative research methods is that we transform ourselves:

1. From a position where scientifically derived knowledge is deemed superior, to a circumstance in which *artistic and intuitive knowledge may be equally appropriate*
2. From an a priori instrumental view of knowledge, to one that *reflects knowledge as being tentative and problematic*
3. From a view that presupposes answers to complex social questions, to one which *endorses the importance of problem posing and negotiated resolution* (Smyth, 1989, p. 7)

In other words, the world for the qualitative researcher is tentative, problematic, and ever changing. Many qualitative researchers see research as participatory, dialogic, transformative, and educative. In this text, I am using the metaphor of stretching and dance as an art form to illuminate some of the many components of qualitative work; observation skills, interview skills, and the role of the researcher skills help one to arrive at that level of participation, transformation, and education.

There is a long and embedded theoretical history urging me to start with the work of John Dewey (1934/1958) on *Art as Experience*. In fact, for Dewey, art was not about daydreaming but about providing a sense of the whole of something, much the same way qualitative researchers see the whole picture in their slice of the case under study. In *The Early Works*, Dewey (1967) states,

> The poet not only detects subtler analogies than other (men), and provides the subtler link of identity where others see confusion and difference, but the form of his expression, his language, images, etc. are controlled by deeper unities ... of feeling. The objects, ideas, connected are perhaps remote from each other to the intellect, but feeling fuses them. Unity of feeling gives artistic unity, wholeness of effect, to the composition. (p. 96)

So for Dewey, especially in *The Early Works*, imagination was highly valued and was explained in terms of feeling. In 1931, when Dewey delivered the first of the William James lectures at Harvard, the subject was that which became *Art as Experience*. He was roundly criticized at the time. Most problematic was Dewey's suggestion that art is about communication and about experience. Dewey refused to separate art from ordinary experience. He said that the artist should "restore continuity between the refined and intensified forms of experience that are works of art and the everyday events, doings, and sufferings that are universally recognized to constitute experience" (Dewey, 1934/1958, p. 3).

I beg the reader's indulgence here as I try to make the ordinary activities described in this text evocative of Dewey's notions, in order for the prospective qualitative researcher to eventually become aware of a critical approach to art as experience. This is the only way that makes sense for me, and so bear with me as I interpret Dewey's pragmatism.

Likewise, I layer this view of Dewey's with Elliot Eisner's (1985) artistic approach to education and evaluation. These are interstitial layers, for Eisner's work has been influenced by Dewey's as well. For the purposes of this text, I would like to frame the exercises with Eisner's (1991) well-known features of qualitative study. To refresh the reader's memory they are:

1. Qualitative studies are field focused.
2. Qualitative studies rely on the self as research instrument.
3. Qualitative studies are interpretive in character.
4. Qualitative studies rely on the use of expressive language and the presence of voice in the text.
5. Qualitative studies attend to particulars.
6. Qualitative studies become believable and instructive because of their coherence, insight, and instrumental utility. (see pp. 32-39)

For the purposes of this text, the description and observation exercises relate to the field-focused nature of the work. The role of the researcher exercises relate to the self as research instrument. The interview exercises relate to the interpretive, expressive nature of this work and the presence of voice in the text.

■ Hindsight

Although these exercises are for those who are interested, at the same time, they are not for everyone. Not everyone has tapped into their artistic intelligence. Although I am in agreement with those writers who have found that we all have an artistic side and multiple intelligences (see Howard Gardner's 1993 work), I also have found that the learner must take an active role in discovering one's artistic intelligence. In addition to this active stance, the artistic theoretical frame that drives these exercises is critical, transformative, educative, and ethical. These exercises were created from a lifetime of reading and action. More or less, these writers were part of my dialogue with myself: John Dewey, Elliot Eisner, Myles Horton, Henry Giroux, Maxine Greene, and Paulo Freire. (See Supplemental Readings at the end of this chapter.) Just as the dancer might look before she leaps, so the reader of this text might look with a critical and enlightened eye. I must ask the reader to do something that is very difficult, to give up one view of the world and imagine another.

I also would like to clarify that I am writing in this style purposefully. I chose an accessible, informal, narrative style, in ordinary language and in my voice, for the following reasons:

1. *To disrupt* what some have called academic writing, which not only distances the reader from what is written but also denigrates the reader's experience
2. *To educate and to engage* the reader, who may not, until now, have had an interest in qualitative research
3. *To inspire* the reader to go further and read the writings on theory and practice in qualitative research
4. *To demystify* the research process by the use of ordinary language and thereby open up the pool of researchers in our field
5. *To democratize* the research process. Qualitative research techniques open up the process of research to many more researchers, who take responsibility for the rigor and high standards of this work. Consequently there is less emphasis on only a few elite individuals taking ownership of these approaches.

■ How to Use This Book

The whole idea of this text is to get the reader to stretch. These exercises should get you started in the actual experience of doing observations and conducting interviews. Fieldwork is mostly work, after all. You may wish to scan the book before beginning the exercises. I begin with Observation Exercises in order to force you into another way of thinking about the world. Think of these exercises as making you stronger, more flexible, and more fluid a researcher just as the dancer becomes stronger, more flexible, and more fluid after stretching. There is a regularity and discipline to fieldwork, and these exercises are progressive in difficulty in each of the major sections.

The exercises provide a process for developing skills in the main techniques of qualitative research methods, that is, observations and interviews. The shape of these exercises developed over time and will continue to develop. In dance, there are no static points. Likewise, in qualitative research, there is no static point, only reshaping the movement and continual questioning and analysis. The reader may also notice that many of these exercises refer to the *arts and humanities* in order to broaden the conversation and thinking about the research process. I have always found that my own background in drawing, photography, drama, and dance has provided the foundation for activities that eventually provide access for many students to improve as interviewers and observers of the world. For me, research is alive and active. It is the most exciting use of many ways of looking at the world and interpreting the world. I hope these exercises will convey a portion of that enthusiasm for knowing.

■ The Audience for This Book

This text is for anyone who wants to practice the two most prominent techniques used in qualitative research projects, interviewing and observation techniques. In addition, some exercises included in the text are for the purpose of developing a stronger awareness of the role of the researcher. As an educator, I would include the group of students of research as a major portion of the audience. Colleagues who wish to practice qualitative research methods are certainly included as well. May the reader of this text have a passion for disciplined inquiry, a high tolerance for ambiguity, a rich imagination, an open mind toward ordinary language usage, and a very good sense of humor.

■ Works Cited in This Chapter

Bruss, N., & Macedo, D. (1985). Towards a pedagogy of the question: Conversations with Paulo Freire. *Journal of Education, 167*(2), 7-21.

Dewey, J. (1958). *Art as experience.* New York: Capricorn Books. (Original work published 1934)

Dewey, J. (1967). *The early works.* Carbondale: Southern Illinois University Press.

Eisner, E. (1985). *The educational imagination: On the design and evaluation of school programs* (3rd ed.). New York: Macmillan.

Eisner, E. (1991). *The enlightened eye.* New York: Macmillan.

Gardner, H. (1993). *Multiple intelligences: The theory in practice.* New York: Basic Books.

Glaser, B. G., & Strauss, A. L. (1967). *The discovery of grounded theory: Strategies for qualitative research.* Hawthorne, NY: Aldine.

hooks, b. (1994). *Teaching to transgress.* New York: Routledge.

Janesick, V. J. (1994). The dance of qualitative research design: Metaphor, methodolatry, and meaning. In N. K. Denzin & Y. S. Lincoln (Eds.), *Handbook of qualitative research* (pp. 209-219). Thousand Oaks, CA: Sage.

Smyth, J. (Ed.). (1989). *Critical perspectives on educational leadership.* New York: Falmer.

■ Supplemental Readings

Addams, F., with Horton, M. (1992). *Unearthing seeds of fire: The idea of highlander.* Winston-Salem, NC: John F. Blair.

Crabtree, B. F., Miller, W. L., Addison, R., Gilchrist, V., & Kuzel, A. (Eds.). (1994). *Exploring collaborative research in primary care.* Thousand Oaks, CA: Sage.

Cunningham, M. (1985). *The dancer and the dance.* New York: Marion Boyars.

Denzin, N. K. (1970). *The research act.* Englewood Cliffs, NJ: Prentice Hall.

Denzin, N. K. (1997). *Interpretive ethnography.* Thousand Oaks, CA: Sage.

Dewey, J. (1963). *Experience and education.* New York: Collier. (Original work published 1938)

Dewey, J. (1966). *Democracy and education.* New York: The Free Press. (Original work published 1916)

Eisner, E. W. (1994). *The educational imagination: On the design and evaluation of school programs* (3rd ed.). New York: Macmillan.

Flax, J. (1990). *Thinking fragments: Psychoanalysis, feminism, and postmodernism in the contemporary West.* Berkeley: University of California Press.

Freire, P. (1994). *Pedagogy of hope: Reliving pedagogy of the oppressed.* New York: Continuum.

Giroux, H. A. (1988). *Teachers as intellectuals: Toward a critical pedagogy of learning.* Granby, MA: Bergin & Garvey.

Giroux, H. A. (1992). *Border crossings: Cultural workers and the politics of education.* New York: Routledge.

Giroux, H. A. (1993). *Living dangerously: Multiculturalism and the politics of difference.* New York: Peter Lang.

Giroux, H. A. (1994). *Disturbing pleasures: Learning popular culture.* New York: Routledge.

Giroux, H. A. (1996). *Fugitive cultures: Race, violence, & youth.* New York: Routledge.

Greene, M. (1995). *Releasing the imagination.* San Francisco: Jossey-Bass.
hooks, b. (1995). *Art on my mind: Visual politics.* New York: The New Press.
Van Manen, M. (1990). *Researching lived experience.* Albany: SUNY Press.
Yow, V. (1994). *Recording oral history.* Thousand Oaks, CA: Sage.

PART 2

Observation Exercises ■

Some set great value on method, while others pride themselves on dispensing with method. To be without method is deplorable, but to depend on method entirely is worse. You must first learn to observe the rules faithfully; afterward, modify them according to your intelligence and capacity. The end of all method is to have no method.

Lu Ch'ai

One of my favorite dance teachers in New York City, from the Cunningham School at Westbeth, once asked all of us in class to observe her movement closely. The reason to observe so carefully, she said, "was to become more aware of your own body and mind" and to "internalize" the movement. She emphasized that until we could observe ourselves and each other, we would not be able to dance with freedom. From this, I began to learn that observing carefully was so focused an activity that to teach others to observe, I needed a way to introduce observation practices that allowed the learner to develop skill and adeptness by taking one step at a time. The seven exercises described in this section start out simply and grow in complexity as the learner becomes more practiced in each activity. Again, this is not meant to be done in a slavish following of a recipe. Each person may improvise at any given point, so that the learner continues to claim an active part in the activity. I begin with an exercise taught to me by my favorite high school art teacher, which is simply to observe a group of objects. Although this was originally an exercise for drawing, I find it helpful to introduce prospective researchers to the activity of description. Also, this exercise may help to place observation in a historical context as a step in an ancient and continuing journey. One aim I have for all my work is to understand qualitative inquiry in a historical context that goes back ages in time in order to recognize a common history. I like to frame the history of observation of one's environment beginning in 3000 B.C.E., when the Chinese master painters began recording their observations of everyday moments in their environment with descriptions of trees, orchids, rocks, plants, water, and so on. I arbitrarily start with the Chinese because of their long history of appreciation for nature, observation, and aesthetics and because of their systematic and methodical approach to documentation. Likewise, I stress the meaning of the term *empirical* at this point to reflect its meaning, "relying on direct experience and observation" as the cornerstone of qualitative work.

Exercise 1 ■

Observing a Still Life Scene ■

Purpose: To observe and describe an assortment of objects on a table

Problem: To see these objects from your position in the room

Time: 5 minutes

Activity: Set up a table in the center of the room so that viewers will have multiple positions and vantage points as they observe at least five objects, each of a different shape, texture, size, and color. Select any objects, but, for example, most recently I have used

1. A ceramic vase from China decorated with blue and white herons
2. A standup 5×7 picture frame with the photo of a young woman
3. A textbook

4. A Russian Pepsi bottle with the characters in Russian
5. A coffee mug with familiar University of Kansas logos and a Jayhawk
   mascot imprint

These are placed on a portable table for all to view from their seats. I envision a room with rectangular work tables arranged in a rectangle, which allows for each person to have a direct view of some portion of the scene. If the reader is working on these exercises alone, the reader selects a space for this activity. Space and how it is used are as critical for the qualitative researcher as they are for the dancer.

Aim: In 5 minutes, describe what you see on the table. Use descriptive terms and fieldnote format. Although there are countless ways to take fieldnotes, for the purposes of the group, we all agree to use one format. On the left third of the page is space for the researcher to write notes to him- or herself; the actual descriptive fieldnotes are taken on the right two thirds of the page. In the upper righthand corner, there is space for the following information: date, time, place, and participants. Learners are urged to develop a system of pagination and classification of notes. For example, for descriptions of settings, one may use a color code at the top of the page or may select a different color of paper. For descriptions of interactions in a social setting, another color code at the paper top may be used, and so on. In any event, the object is to encourage learners to create a system of coding that works for them. Figure 2.1 is a sample of a fieldnote page in the format and style we have adopted because it is effective for our purposes.

		Date- 2-9-96
		Time- 3:33 PM
		Place- MX High School
		Participants- JS, PWB

Notes to Myself: Fieldnotes:

I am waiting for JS   I arrive a bit earlier to set up my tape recorder and begin to
to arrive   interview the principal and take notes.
                                            The outer office is filled with action. First there is, . . .

Figure 2.1. A Sample Fieldnote Format

In this exercise to observe objects, the learners take notes as the observation takes place. After 5 minutes, they change seats and observe and describe the objects for another period of 5 minutes. The purpose for doing this is to experience the effects on description of changing seats and viewpoint. Later, we discuss the reactions of the students.

Discussion: 1. How did you approach this exercise in the first 5 minutes? The second 5 minutes? Did you do anything differently in the second observation after you changed seating? Volunteers read their descriptions.

2. What was most difficult for you in this exercise?

Rationale: The questions are designed to discover how learners approach the task and how others approach the same task. Some begin by describing one object at a time from left to right, for example, forgetting to situate themselves in such and such a room. Others begin by describing the room and working their way to the table then to objects. By sharing their personal experience, class members begin to see the wide variety of approaches to the task. They also see which members are skilled at description and which members need to practice more. There is no better teacher than example, so that in class when a skilled observer and describer reads a powerful description to the class, the lesson sinks in.

After all, the researcher is the research instrument and these practice exercises in observation and description are designed to bring home this very point.

Evaluation: In addition to my evaluation of individual work, I ask participants to evaluate themselves. Each is asked to fill out the form shown in Figure 2.2 or to write me a letter and return to discuss it at the beginning of the next class before beginning the next exercise, the observation of the classroom setting. For those working alone, write a letter to someone you trust evaluating this process. I use this form to facilitate an active agency as evaluators of one's work. The questions are meant to be a heuristic tool and a starting point for the evaluative process. Most often, I ask learners to keep a journal of all their thoughts related to the class and these activities. Although many are intimidated by writing a journal, this can be a good evaluation tool and a valuable historical document for charting the role of the researcher in

---

Evaluation of _____ (name the exercise), Date_____

a. Things I learned about myself as I described the objects under observation:

b. Things I need to continue to work on for the next observation:

c. How I describe my progress:

Figure 2.2. A Sample Formative Evaluation

a given project. Journal writing is my first choice and suggestion for self-reflection and evaluation. Of course, the point is to allow the individual to become a stakeholder in self-evaluation.

This baptism into self-evaluation continues with each practice exercise and is part of an overall system of self-evaluation that is depicted in Figure 2.3.

■ **Constructing a Reflective Portfolio**

Individuals build a portfolio throughout the semester of their own work and self-evaluation of their work. This allows for the opportunity to evaluate externally and internally, a requirement for the qualitative researcher. To create and shape an individual portfolio, I ask learners to bring in a notebook or folder with their photo attached to it, and each week we add to the portfolio as needed. This also affords the opportunity to review and monitor the notebooks on a regular and sustained basis. Using what we learned from the still life description, we move on to the next level of complexity, description of a setting.

A summative evaluation allows you to rate yourself at this point in time, given all the observations completed to date. Keep a log of the type of observation you completed, the date completed, and time, place, and participants involved as applicable. Try to chart your progress from the first observation exercise to the final one. On a scale of 1 to 10, 10 being the highest rating, rate yourself overall, and list three reasons why you gave yourself this particular rating.

To help you get started, look at these basic questions in your rating system.

1. What was your purpose on this observation and did you achieve it?
2. How do you know that you achieved your purpose?
3. Would you change anything about your observation skills at this point? Describe and explain.
4. What was your stance as a researcher as you completed these exercises?
5. What prior knowledge or theory can you draw upon to explain your skill as an observer?
6. What readings helped you come to this level of understanding and expertise?
7. If you were to continue practicing this particular skill, how and in what ways would you continue?

Now you have some basic tools for summative evaluation of the observation cycle. You may also want to apply this to the interview exercises and the role of the researcher exercises.

Figure 2.3. A Summative Evaluation for This Cycle

Exercise 2 ■

Physical Description of This Setting ■

Purpose: To observe one section of the room we are seated in

Problem: To see this section of the room

Time: 5 minutes

Activity: Select a section of this room that is immediately across from where you are seated. Describe this section of the room in detail.

Evaluation: Continue with self-evaluation and overall evaluation for your portfolio.

Discussion: 1. How did you approach this exercise?
            2. How is this exercise like the previous exercise? Unlike?
            3. What was the most difficult part of this activity?

Rationale: The movement from a still life description to the setting is a step in complexity. Now the learner is faced with a number of additional possibilities in how to approach this assignment and how to execute it. Beginning the journey to becoming a better observer includes this challenge, which is to describe a large physical area. Some individuals add a floor plan and rough sketch of the setting, only to return later and measure the floor, the room, the furniture, and so on. Others may take a photo of the setting. Later, the learner tries to capture in narrative form what was captured in the drawing or the photograph.

Exercise 3 ■

Observation in the Home or Workplace ■

Purpose: To continue developing observation skill with a setting. Observe an area in your home or workplace.

Problem: To see your own space as you never have before

Time: 30 minutes

Activity: Select an area that is part of your living and/or working space to observe and describe. Set aside 30 minutes of peace and quiet time to describe a portion of your room or office. Set reasonable goals of description. For example, select one half of the room to describe or one section of the office, and so on. Again, after taking notes, type them in fieldnote format and return to class with these data.

Discussion: In class, we will share our descriptions and frame our discussion around the following questions:

1. How did you approach this description of a setting?
2. How did this differ from the previous exercise in class?
3. What was the most difficult part of this exercise for you?

Evaluation: Continue with self-evaluation and overall evaluation for your portfolio.

Rationale: By this time, individuals have completed two observation exercises and now move to another level. The learner has a wider band of options to reflect and act upon. Will I select home or workplace to describe? Once selected, which area of the site will I focus on? With the luxury of 30 minutes of observation time, how do I use this time to my best advantage? All are encouraged to think about how this exercise goes beyond both the description of a still life arrangement and description of the classroom.

Exercise 4 ■

Description of a Familiar Person ■

Purpose: To describe a person sitting across from oneself

Problem: To see someone as never before

Time: 15 minutes

Activity: Select a person to describe physically. Arrange your 15 minutes again, to your best advantage. Remember to use descriptive terms and work for accuracy.

Discussion: 1. What can you identify as major differences in observation of a still life, a setting, and a person?
2. How did you approach this exercise?
3. What was difficult for you in this exercise and what do you want to do about it?
4. Is there anything about description of a person that relates to your role as the researcher?

Evaluation: Continue with self-evaluation and overall evaluation for your portfolio.

Rationale: The shift from describing objects and settings to describing people is a major shift. For one thing, people are animated. Previous to this, learners had an inanimate, static environment to describe. Now

learners must move to another complicating factor in their observation practice, the factor of activity, movement, and life. This exercise
is designed to prepare them for observations of people in their future
projects.

Exercise 5 ■

Observing a Stranger ■

Purpose: To observe and describe a person who is a stranger to the observer

Problem: To see this person and describe them

Time: 15 minutes

Activity: Take time to select a person in a public space such as the student union, the library, a dormitory, or a coffee shop and ask them if you
may observe and describe them for 15 minutes. Introduce yourself
and explain that you are doing this to become a better observer. As-
sure them of confidentiality and that no harm will come to them. If a
person refuses, go on to find another person who is willing to be observed. After 15 minutes of observation, return to the group (if you
have the benefit of a class, for example) to discuss this experience. If
on your own, take a few minutes to write down your thoughts about
this exercise.

Discussion: 1. Identify what you were thinking as you approached the person you
selected for an interview.
2. How did this differ from observing someone you knew?
3. What was most difficult for you in this activity?

Evaluation: Continue with self-evaluation and overall evaluation.

Rationale: Learners move to yet another level when they begin to realize what it
is like to approach a stranger to observe. They begin to realize what
gaining access and entry to a social setting feels like, although admit-

tedly they are in a safe environment, at this point, and one that is somewhat familiar to them. In addition, learners have firsthand experience in articulating their goals of observation.

Exercise 6 ■

Observing an Animal at Home, ■
the Zoo, or a Pet Shop

Purpose: To describe an animal at home or at the zoo

Problem: To see and recognize the complexity of the animal's movement

Activity: Go to the zoo or a pet shop or observe an animal in your household. Physically describe the animal, how the animal eats, moves, and shifts position and attention.

  Can you make a list of five adjectives that describe this animal? Do you see inner qualities as well as outer qualities? Isolate your description to include limbs, eyes, head, mannerisms. Find two traits of the animal that you also find in human beings. Construct a metaphor for this animal. (Two examples are provided in Figure 2.4.)

Time: Take as much time as you like with the observation.

Discussion: 1. What did you notice about yourself as an observer as you began this exercise?
  2. What was difficult about describing an animal?

Evaluation: Continue with self-evaluation and overall evaluation for your portfolio.

Rationale: Individuals may learn something about the difficulty of observing people by beginning with observation of animals. Like human beings, animals are animated, unpredictable, and active. This is a good beginning step in complex description in a complex setting. Learners often remark that although difficult, this exercise was challenging and enjoyable at the same time.

Exercise 7 ■

Nonparticipant Observation Assignment ■

Place: Restaurant, coffee shop, shopping mall, zoo, place of worship, museum, or any public setting

Purpose: To observe a complex public setting. There should be natural public access to the setting and multiple viewing opportunities for you.

Activity: Nonparticipant observation. Go to this social setting more than once to get a sense of the complexity and to maximize what you learn. Go at least three times at different times of the day. If you wish to return at any other time, of course, feel free to do so. Take notes. Make a floor plan. See what you are able to hear, see, and learn just by observing.

What to look for:
1. The Setting: Look around you and describe the entire physical space. Draw a floor plan or take a photo if permitted.
2. The People: Look around you and describe the people in this setting. Focus on one or two of the people. What are they doing in that social space?
3. The Action: What are the relationships between people and/or groups? Try to discover something about the people in the setting.
4. Describe the groups and any common characteristics, for example, age, gender, dress codes, speech, activity, and so on.
5. Focus on one person in your viewing area to describe in detail. For example, a waitress, a caretaker, a salesperson, and so on, depending on your setting.
6. If you had all the time in the world to do a study here, what three things would you look for upon returning to the setting?

Time: You have 3 weeks to complete this assignment. Be sure to include a self-evaluation.

Discussion:
1. Of all the exercises so far, how has this one challenged you?
2. How did you approach this assignment?
3. What difficulties did you encounter in the field setting?
4. What would you do differently if you were to return?

Description of a Cat

This cat I am looking at is more like a small farm animal than what I think of as a cat. This cat is pure white fluff and in fact the fur over her eyes nearly obscures the strangely yellow eyeballs. She is part watermelon and part turtle for she waddles as she walks carrying a huge load around her middle section.

I am seated on the sofa in a friend's living room and as I try to write some descriptive notes here, I wonder why he adores this cat. As the cat arranges herself on the throw rug, she stretches and curls up half way, completely falling asleep. I see her heavy breathing in terms of the belly roll going up and down like waves. I continue to observe this and she remains still except for breathing.

My five adjectives for the cat are: large, snowy, listless, sleepy, and contented. The inner quality she displayed in her walk seems to be imperviousness. She owns the room and the rug and is not even concerned that I am watching her. Her name is Fifi. She does not respond to the name when I call her. She is ignoring me, I am afraid.

I can only see the round midsection, which looks like a rock in the living room. I guess she is about 40 pounds and about 16 inches long and at least 14 inches wide! She sneezes twice and as she does this, her body curls up into itself a bit and then elongates again. She seems to have the human qualities of boredom and laziness. This cat is a con artist.

I have observed about 15 minutes. Can I return and try to describe her again?

Description of a Gorilla

This gorilla I am observing belongs to the family of anthropoid apes of western equatorial Africa related to the chimpanzee but less erect and much bigger in size. What strikes me immediately about this gorilla, whose name is Pavarotti, is how remarkably human he is. His fur, for example, is a deep rich ebony with brownish streaks, and he moves his hair about as he rubs his stomach or his leg alternately. I wonder what that means.

I see why they call him Pavarotti for he seems to be singing or at least communicating something with high-pitched grunts and moans. Not quite yodeling but somewhat close to that. He puffs his chest forward and struts a bit.

There are five of us observing him, and he seems to be aware of this. (Am I imagining this because he is so human in movement?) I see him in these 10 minutes jump from platform to rope to tree branch and landing on a thick branch. Then he sits down cross-legged on the V formation of the tree, which becomes his seat. He then lifts his elbow onto his knee and places his right hand under his chin, sitting like "The Thinker," only cross-legged. Then he takes a look at his fingernails and starts cleaning the fingernails of the left hand, which leads me to think he is right-handed. He also favors his right arm when he swings, and I notice his expressive face. I seem to think he is laughing, then frowning, then laughing again. Is this an act? Did he design this show?

Five adjectives that describe him are energetic, human, whimsical, daunting, and brave. His inner qualities seem to be awareness of observers, recognition of our intrusion of our space. Two traits he displays are bravado and cleanliness. I think this gorilla is an actor.

I want to go back at least twice, maybe three times, to describe more carefully the hands and feet, which seem almost identically human.

Figure 2.4. Examples of Descriptions

Evaluation: Continue self-evaluation and at this point, you need to complete a summative evaluation for this cycle, the observation cycle.

Rationale: At this point, the individual has direct experience in nonparticipant observation, observation, and self-evaluation and has been given the opportunity to discuss with peers progress to date. These exercises give learners a taste of what it will be like in the field, in terms of the ministudy for the class and quite possibly for their own dissertation or future research activities. Also, there is a growth in terms of thinking like a researcher and developing a role for oneself. In the context of a course, the ministudy in the course may be used as a pilot study for a dissertation project if it is reasonable to do so. No matter what the situation of the individual reader of this text, throughout the practice of these exercises, learners must continue reading from a series of reading lists. (See Appendix O for samples of completed projects.)

■ Next Steps

The next three protocols show some possibilities for becoming an active agent as researcher. The learner takes responsibility for self-evaluation, as in the sample, Figure 2.5, Self-Evaluation Per Exercise. The option of Figure 2.6, My Story to the Best of My Knowledge, allows for a more introspective turn. Finally, Figure 2.7, Model Format to explain Your Study, should be seen as a working document, a starting point for the learner to begin constructing the ministudy that brings together the practice of and learning from all of these exercises at this point. Those who prefer letter writing to any of the sample forms I have provided may write a letter to themselves or to me, describing what they learned from this assignment. Now the learner moves on to the cycle of interviewing.

■ Summary of Part 2: The Observation Cycle

In this series of seven exercises, the learner has direct experience in observation of a still life, a physical setting, people, and an

Self-Evaluation of my _____ activity.
List three adjectives that describe what you learned from this activity.
   1.
   2.
   3.

Locate Yourself!
Historically, the theory/theories that have most affected me and shaped me are (list at least 3 authors). Explain.
   1.
   2.
   3.

The reason these authors have shaped my thinking is:

Figure 2.5. Self-Evaluation Per Exercise

In this exercise, I want you to reflect on your intellectual growth and development. Which ideas have dazzled you? Prompted you to go further in your studies?
   Try to remember at least one to three incidents from school, kindergarten to the present, that have profoundly affected your thinking. Describe in detail these incidents, sights, sounds, smells, tastes, feel of them, key participants, your own memory of how you reacted at the time, and how you view this today. Add this entry to your portfolio.

Name_____ Date_____

Incident One:

Incident Two:

Incident Three:

Figure 2.6. My Story to the Best of My Knowledge

animal, as well as performing a nonparticipant observation activity. The exercises move forward with increasing complexity in sharpening one's observation skills. All are encouraged to evaluate their own progress as they move through the exercise cycle. All evaluate their own progress for each individual activity and then

1. The purpose of this study is to describe and explain:
   (example: the belief system of an educational leader)
2. The theory that guides the study is:
   (example: Symbolic Interactionism)
3. The exploratory questions that guide the study include:
   a. What elements or characteristics make up this leader's beliefs about education?
   b. What variables influence this set of beliefs?
4. The literature related to this study includes:
   a. methodology literature
      (name the area)
   b. topical literature
      (name the area)

Figure 2.7. Model Format to Explain Your Study

complete a summative evaluation statement on their own progress overall, as an observer. This series of exercises is seen as preparation for progressing to the next cycle of exercise, the interviewing exercises. Again, learners have the opportunity to actively engage in interviewing exercises as described in Part 3. Furthermore, these exercises have their origin in the arts and humanities.

■ Pitfalls and Guidelines

Learners who have the luxury of a class situation or a community of scholars to discuss daily progress have offered the following advice on these observation exercises:

1. Focus and concentration are the critical elements to doing a decent observation.
2. Overdoing it, that is overdescribing one piece of a setting, for example, may hamper the end result.
3. Underdescribing could harm the overall effect and goal of the exercise, if not enough attention is paid to each component of the exercise. When in doubt, keep writing and refining those observation skills.

Because of the hectic pace of many of our lives, being still long enough to observe and describe a setting, an object, or a person requires an observer to settle down and become totally absorbed in the given activity. Most learners seem to get better at this the more they do it. In this case, practice really does allow the individual to improve and proceed in the series. Like the dancer in training who improves through consistent, relentless, and disciplined exercise, the qualitative researcher in training may improve as an observer of the human condition.

■ Supplemental Readings

Readings that may help you in understanding the observation process are listed below. Select a variety of writers. Find the writer who speaks to you. There is no end to information in the library. Be sure to allot time for a library search and physically take yourself there. Promise me this!

Always check *Dissertation Abstracts* for the latest examples of completed projects using qualitative methods in your field.

Denzin, N. K., & Lincoln, Y. S. (1994). *Handbook of qualitative research.* Thousand Oaks, CA: Sage.

Eisner, E. *The enlightened eye.* (1991). New York: Macmillan.

Marshall, C., & Rossman, G. B. (1989). *Designing qualitative research.* Thousand Oaks, CA: Sage.

Powdermaker, H. (1966). *Stranger and friend: The way of the anthropologist.* New York: Norton.

Spradley, J. (1980). *Participant observation.* New York: Holt, Rinehart & Winston.

Stake, R. E. (1995). *The art of case study research.* Thousand Oaks, CA: Sage.

Strauss, A., & Corbin, J. (1990). *Qualitative research methods.* Thousand Oaks, CA: Sage.

Van Manen, M. (1990). *Researching lived experience.* New York: SUNY Press.

Wolcott, H. (1994). *Transforming qualitative data.* Thousand Oaks, CA: Sage.

Yow, V. (1994). *Recording oral history.* Thousand Oaks, CA: Sage.

PART 3

The Interview Cycle ■

Spoon feeding in the long run teaches us nothing but the shape
of the spoon.

E. M. Forster

Probably the most rewarding component of any qualitative
research project is interviewing. Whereas observation is the
act of taking notice of something, interviewing is an act of communication. In fact, a major contribution to our history as qualitative
researchers is the growing contribution in the literature about
solid interviewing techniques. Since at least the 1930s, we have
seen a remarkable and serious interest in research interviewing.
(See Janesick, 1991; Lazarsfeld, 1935; Metzler, 1989; Mishler, 1986;
Riesman, 1956; Spradley, 1979.) I consider this a tremendous leap
forward in that interviews provide such rich and substantive data
for the researcher and are also a major part of qualitative research
work. I have written earlier about the importance of interviews
and ways of approaching them. I would like to frame this chapter
in terms of some of those earlier key points, which I will summarize here. A good deal of what I have learned about interviewing
ultimately came from trial and error within long-term interview
studies. This chapter is meant to be a nonthreatening and systematic way to approach the very complex and challenging act of
interviewing another person.

■ Two People Talking, Communication, and Constructing Meaning

Interviewing is an ancient technique and for the purposes of this text, I define it in this way:

> Interviewing is a meeting of two persons to exchange information and ideas through questions and responses, resulting in communication and joint construction of meaning about a particular topic.

As we are always researchers in the process of conducting a study, we rely on different kinds of questions for eliciting various responses. Spradley (1979) suggested three types of questions for interviewing that have always worked for me: descriptive, contrasting, and structural questions. I have been inspired as well by Mishler (1986) in the process of teaching about interviews, and expanding these notions, I offer the following as examples of types of interview questions:

■ Types of Interview Questions

1. *Basic Descriptive Questions*

   Can you talk to me about your car accident? Tell me what happened on that evening. Describe how you felt that evening.

2. *Follow-up Questions*

   You mentioned that "planning time" is important to you. Can you tell me how you use planning time?

3. *Experience/Example Questions*

   You mentioned that you loved going to Paris. Can you give me an example or two of what made you love Paris? Talk about your impressions of Paris.

4. *Simple Clarification Questions*

   You have used the term *constructivist teacher* today. Can you clarify that for me? What exactly can you tell me about your constructivist teaching?

5. *Structural/Paradigmatic Questions*

   You stated that this class was a problematic one. What would you describe as the cause of these problems?

Of all the things you have told me about being a critical care nurse, what is the underlying premise of your workday? In other words, what keeps you going every day?

6. *Comparison/Contrast Questions*

You said there was a big difference between a great principal and an ordinary principal. What are some of these differences? Can you describe a few for me?

■ Preparing Questions

A good rule of thumb for interviewing is to be prepared. Compose as many thoughtful questions as possible. It is far better to be overprepared rather than to get caught in an interview without questions. Usually five or six questions of the type described above may yield well over an hour of interview data on tape. A simple question like, "Tell me about your day as a cocktail waitress," once yielded nearly 2 hours of interview data, leaving all the other questions for another interview time. You will learn to develop a sense of awareness about your participants in the study and rearrange accordingly. To prepare for testing out some of the questions you create, let us proceed to some exercises that will give you some experience with interviewing. In this section of the text, all the interview exercises will follow the following format.

1. First, be prepared with tape recorder, tape, and a notebook to take fieldnotes while interviewing.
2. Before the interview, check your recorder and tape to see that both are functional. Test your voice on the tape by saying the *date, time, place,* and *the name of the participant* on the tape. This is helpful later, not only when you do the transcriptions of the tape but also for jarring your memory at a subsequent date.
3. Whenever possible, carry a spare tape recorder and extra tapes and batteries. Many cases have been described where the tape was malfunctioning, the recorder died, and or the batteries wore out.
4. If you feel more comfortable with giving a copy of the interview questions to your participant, do so ahead of time.
5. Call ahead as a reminder and verify the exact date, time, and place of the interview and arrive early.

Exercise 1 ▪

Interviewing Someone You Know ▪

Find someone you know to interview on any one of the following topics for 20 minutes.

1. What are your beliefs about friendship?

or

2. Describe for me someone you totally admire, either a historical figure or someone alive today. Explain why you selected this person and why you admire this person.

or

3. Describe your typical workday from the moment you arise in the morning to the end of your day.

Be sure to tape your interview and take fieldnotes to train yourself to observe nonverbal cues and behaviors.

Discussion: 1. How did you approach this exercise?
2. What was most difficult for you?
3. Would you change anything the next time you interview someone?

Learners now get a chance to practice working with taped interview data by transcribing at least a portion of, if not the entire, interview. Later, the group will practice analyzing data from these interviews in groups, with partners, or alone, as they see fit.

Evaluation: Learners follow the same evaluation exercises as in the previous chapter, keeping track of their progress and reflecting on the meaning of the exercise.

Exercise 2 ■

Interviewing a Stranger ■

Learners follow the same directions as above, only now they must find a stranger to interview. In the class setting, learners go out on campus and find someone. If you are trying this on your own, use your imagination to find someone in the workplace or a public place and interview that person on any of the topics listed above.

Learners are asked to discuss in small groups or in the group at large what was learned from this exercise in comparison to the previous one. Usually, learners find interviewing a stranger easier than interviewing a classmate, neighbor, or colleague. The use of a tape recorder is new to learners at first but becomes second nature once they get over the novelty.

Exercise 3 ■

Phone Interviews ■

At times, a learner may need to do a phone interview in an emergency, to jump-start a project as a preinterview, or to actually rely on a phone interview. Although this has many drawbacks, the chief being that face-to-face communication is not possible, if one has to use this technique, please practice ahead of time. One good idea for practice is to phone someone you know and interview that person on the topic of your choice. If one has a class situation, classmates can phone each other and interview each other on any of the sample topics listed in Exercise 1 or create a list of questions on a given topic.

Be sure to take notes on the phone interview. Overall student reaction to phone interviews is not as positive as a face-to-face interview. There is a more formal, businesslike feel to a phone interview, and consequently, a gap exists in the type of data one can retrieve from such an interview. In any event, if one has to do this, be sure to be prepared, be clear about the purpose of the interview, and leave an opening for the interviewee to add additional information with a question like:

1. Is there anything you wish to add to our conversation today?
2. Is there anything I have forgotten to ask and which you feel is important?

Some Rules of Thumb: Learners who are new to interviews often find it hard to conclude the interview, whether in person or on the phone. When I asked students in hindsight what they suggested as far as concluding interviews, here were the major responses.

1. Be aware of time. Stop when you promised to stop. Rather than let an interview go on and on, make an appointment for a new time.
2. Ask for any papers, documents, or artifacts that have been mentioned in the interview.
3. Leave the window open for future contact. Ask if you may return or call back if something isn't clear to you, the interviewer.
4. Always follow common courtesy and thank the interviewee. In many cases, learners offer to take the person out for coffee or lunch. This is an individual preference, but it does make the interview situation more humane and may help to establish rapport, trust, and communication.

■ About Focus Groups

■ Forms, Uses, Strengths, and Weaknesses

The focus group technique is one of the most common approaches to research in the social sciences. A focus group is a group interview, with a trained moderator, a specific set of questions, and a disciplined approach to studying ideas in a group context. The data from the focus group is the typed transcript of the group interaction.

■ History

Focus groups originated in sociology, but most current applications are in marketing research to test products or in political science to test issues with voters. In the 1940s, focus groups were used by sociologists to study wartime propaganda and its effects. Merton (1987) extended his earlier work in this area. About 40 years later, focus group work began anew and was used in medical studies (see Gubrium, 1987) regarding heart problems and Alzheimer's disease. Political handlers use this technique regularly to the present day. How can we forget the last presidential campaign and the relentless references to focus groups? Likewise, communications, business, anthropology, and sociology are fields that make use of focus groups. Increasingly, educational researchers are using focus groups as well.

■ Uses and Ways to View Focus Groups

    1. Self-contained research technique

or

    2. Supplemental technique for qualitative and/or quantitative studies (see Morgan, 1988)

Focus groups are useful for:

    1. Orienting oneself to a new field
    2. Generating hypotheses based on a person's insight
    3. Evaluating different research sites or study populations
    4. Getting participants' interpretations of results from earlier studies
    5. Getting feedback from participants where there is a power differential, that is, getting information from people who are not in power positions
    6. Getting data about complex behavior
    7. Exposing professionals to the language and culture of a target group, that is, the focus group bridges the gap between the professional and the real world target group

■ Strengths

1. The major strength of focus groups is the use of *the group interaction to produce data that would not be as easily accessible without the group interaction.*
2. Focus groups combine elements of both individual interviews and participant observation, the two principal data collection techniques of qualitative researchers.
3. One can observe a great deal of interaction in a given limited time period on a particular topic.
4. Participants' interaction among themselves replaces the interaction with the interviewer, leading to a greater understanding of participants' points of view.

■ Trade-offs/Disadvantages

1. Focus groups are fundamentally unnatural social settings, when compared to participant observation.
2. Focus groups are often limited to verbal behavior.
3. Focus groups depend on a skilled moderator, not always available when needed.
4. Do not use focus groups if the intent is something other than research; for example, conflict resolution, consensus building, staff retreats, and work to change attitudes.

■ A Sample Approach to Focus Groups

1. Planning Phase: Four weeks

   Be sure to allow planning time. *Identify your goals.* State precisely what is the group focus in one sentence if possible.
2. Identify Members: Four weeks

   (Actual list and backup list) Always have a backup list for last-minute absentees.
3. Two groups per week: Six weeks.

   Members and moderators burn out easily. The logistics of focus group planning, picking up participants if need be, and scheduling a site are often overwhelming. Thus, we found that no more than two groups per week allowed us to be true to our study.
4. Transcripts: Eight weeks

   Note: Transcripts are a most difficult and time-consuming task, and we often underestimated the time we needed for completion. Through experience with the drug-free schools case, we learned to allow 3 to 6 months per project, all conditions being favorable and with few people backing out of the focus group.

After you identify your goals, here are some rules of thumb that were constructed after polling our participants in the project:

1. Three or four groups seem most worthwhile, especially from a moderator's point of view, in a large-scale study.
2. At least two groups are good for exploratory projects.
3. At least six groups seem ideal if detailed content analysis is needed on an unknown topic with relatively unstructured questions.
4. The more homogeneous the group, the fewer you need.

■ Dilemmas

Again, these dilemmas arose from the actual case:

1. Who brings up controversial issues? The moderator or the group?
2. How far does informed consent go if unusually personal information is revealed?

In working for specificity, depth, and understanding of the social context in a given study, the intent of the moderator is always to "get the story." At the same time, with the sensitive topic of alcohol use and drug use as in this case, a fine line between getting the story and walking into privacy issues was always present. On the other hand, we did not want to invest such a great deal of time in a project and ask only superficial questions. We found that a skilled moderator is essentially the key to a successful focus group.

■ Some Myths About Focus Groups

1. Focus groups are quick and cheap.
2. Focus groups must consist of strangers.
3. People will not talk about sensitive issues in groups.
4. Focus groups tend to produce conformity.
5. Focus groups must be validated by other methods.

The following checklist was developed and modified from experience and a combination of the Morgan (1988) and Krueger (1988) texts for the purpose of assisting learners in this process.

Advance Notice

1. Contact participants by phone 1 to 2 weeks before the session.
2. Send each participant a letter of invitation.
3. Give a reminder phone call prior to the session.
4. Slightly overrecruit the number of participants.

Questions

1. The introductory question should be answered quickly and not identify status.
2. Questions should flow in a logical sequence.
3. Use probe questions as needed.
4. Limit the use of "Why" questions.
5. Use "think back" questions as needed.

Logistics

1. The room should be comfortable and a satisfactory size, with tables, and so on.
2. The moderator arrives early.
3. Background noise should not interfere with the tape.
4. Have name tags for everyone.
5. A remote microphone should be placed on the table.
6. Bring extra tapes, batteries, extensions, supplies.
7. Plan topics for small-talk conversation.
8. Seat experts and loud participants near the moderator.
9. Seat shy and quiet participants across from the moderator.
10. When having a meal, limit selection and get to business.
11. Bring enough copies of handouts, visual aids, storyboards, and so on.

Moderator Skills

1. Be well rested, alert, prepared.
2. Practice introduction without referring to notes.

3. Remember questions without referring to notes.
4. Be cautious to avoid head nodding.
5. Avoid comments that signal approval, such as "great," "excellent," and so on, or disapproval.
6. Avoid giving your personal opinion.

Immediately After the Session

1. Prepare a brief summary of key points.
2. Check to see that the tape recorder captured everything.
3. Get tapes to transcriber or begin immediately.
4. Check your fieldnotes as a check and balance tool, and keep a list of all participants' names, addresses, phone numbers, and so on.

Exercise 4 ■

The Focus Group Interview ■

Some learners are anxious to use focus groups as a qualitative research technique, given the nature of the purposes of their study, time line for the study, and resources. Focus groups are not a panacea but do offer a way for researchers to *focus* on a topic with a given group. I ask learners to immediately read at least one text on focus groups, usually the text *Successful Focus Groups,* edited by David Morgan (1993). I use this exercise when I am fortunate enough to be working on a funded project that allows for learner participation. When on a funded project, I involve all students who volunteer to work at the actual sites. If not working on a funded project, learners may benefit from this *demonstration exercise.* This exercise emerged from an actual case of a study we did of the drug-free schools program in northeast Kansas. The topic is one learners and community members can talk about because everyone has something to say about drug use in a given community. For this demonstration focus group, I ask for volunteers.

Topic: Drug availability in your school, community, and neighborhood.

Purpose: To find out how students, teachers, and parents feel about drug use and drug education in your school.

Sample   Note: These questions may be modified for each focus group made
Questions up of parents, teachers, and students. These were the basic ques-
for the   tions used by the trained moderator of the groups, which were rear-
Moderator ranged according to the composition of the group.

1. Can you talk about whether or not you feel safe in your school or community?
2. Do you have some thoughts on how your school or community is doing regarding alcohol and drug problems with students? Can you describe for me what you know about this?
3. What does your school or community do to educate you about the use of alcohol and drugs?
4. Do you think drugs or alcohol are easily available to students?
5. What kinds of rules do you have about alcohol and drugs?
6. If you ever had a problem with alcohol or drugs, who would you approach to talk about it? Can you explain your thoughts about your choice of this individual?
7. Can you talk about your thoughts on how alcohol and drugs affect a person, a family, a school, a community?

In this demonstration exercise, I ask for a volunteer for the moderator who must keep the group on task. Also, I give out role-taking cards with a role for each of the seven volunteers for the focus group. The learners draw a card at random, and here are some of the roles taken by participants.

Card 1: Play yourself.
Card 2: Play yourself.
Card 3: Play disagreeable and refuse to answer every other question.
Card 4: Play overly agreeable and agree with everyone.
Card 5: Say as little as possible and speak only when asked a direct question by the moderator.
Card 6: Say nothing regarding drugs and talk about every and any other subject.
Card 7: Try everything you can to get out of answering any question and keep asking to leave the group.

These seven "types" can be found from time to time in any given focus group in the real world, which is why I have designed these roles partially to train moderators and partially to allow learners to see that focus groups require a great deal of patience, fortitude, tact and diplomacy, and tenacity. Some warnings about focus groups include being ready to deal with people who cry in the group, people who may lose their temper or composure, argumentative members, and so on. If a moderator finds a situation where things get problematic, one can stop the group to take time out and then make a decision about continuing on or not. Thus, moderators need a bit of training in dealing with the public and must have at least the semblance of calm.

Exercise 5 ■

Analyzing Interview Data ■

After the experience of interviewing, learners appreciate the opportunity to practice individually and in groups the demanding task of analyzing interview data. Within the parameters of the class, members have already taped the interview on views of friendship. They transcribe the 10 minutes of tape and then begin working in groups of three or four to find major categories from the data. This is a seemingly small task, yet it takes about an hour of class time. Members go through the transcripts and each other's fieldnotes and listen to the tape as often as they need. Each group comes up with a set of major and minor categories. Remarks after this exercise often include the following:

1. I was amazed at how the categories popped out of the data.
2. This was harder than I thought because I forgot to take fieldnotes during the interview, and so I really needed to know the nonverbals.
3. This was much easier when I had someone to check my categories with. Now I know why having an outside reader of fieldnotes and transcripts, as suggested, is a good idea.
4. This teaches me to have another interview and get more data.
5. The person I interviewed taught me better questions to ask.
6. As I looked over the transcripts, I realized how much I had already forgotten about the focus group. Now I know I have to transcribe everything because my memory is not what it used to be.

After the experience of working on transcripts in the small group, members feel more confident in dealing with their miniprojects as far as analysis of data. Learners look for major themes, key words, and indices of behavior and belief, and they make an initial list of major and minor categories. Every attempt is made to look for critical incidents, points of tension and conflict, and contradictions to help in the purposes of study. In the class situation, most students found working with a group or with a partner to be helpful and illuminating.

■ **Summary and Pitfalls**

In most cases, interviewing is like a duet or pas-de-deux in dance. Two people are communicating with one another and, ideally at least, understand each other whatever the context. The major pitfall in interviewing is not being prepared with mechanical materials, questions, and good communication skills. Direct experience, practice, and reflection are the strongest assets of the interviewer and the dancer.

■ **Works Cited in This Chapter**

Gubrium, J. F. (1987). *Oldtimers and Alzheimer's: The descriptive organization of senility.* Greenwich, CT: JAI Press.

Janesick, V. J. (1991). Ethnographic inquiry: Understanding culture and experience. In E. C. Short (Ed.), *Forms of curriculum inquiry* (pp. 101-119). Albany: SUNY Press.

Krueger, R. A. (1988). *Focus groups: A practical guide for applied research.* Newbury Park, CA: Sage.

Lazarsfeld, P. (1935). The art of asking why: Three principles underlying the formulation of questionnaires. *National Marketing Review, 1,* 1-7.

Merton, R. K. (1987). The focused interview and focus groups: Continuities and discontinuities. *Public Opinion Quarterly, 51,* 550-556.

Metzler, K. (1989). *Creative interviewing.* Englewood Cliffs, NJ: Prentice Hall.

Mishler, E. G. (1986). *Research interviewing: Context and narrative.* Cambridge, MA: Harvard University Press.

Morgan, D. (1988). *Focus groups as qualitative research.* Newbury Park, CA: Sage.

Riesman, D. (1956). Asking and answering. *Journal of Business of the University of Chicago, 29*, 225-236.

Spradley, J. P. (1979). *The ethnographic interview.* New York: Holt, Rinehart & Winston.

■ Supplemental Readings

Fetterman, D. M. (1989). *Ethnography step by step.* Newbury Park, CA: Sage.

Krueger, R. A. (1988). *Focus groups: A practical guide for applied research* Newbury Park, CA: Sage.

Kvale, S. (1996). *InterViews: An introduction to qualitative research interviewing.* Thousand Oaks, CA: Sage.

McCracken, G. (1988). *The long interview.* Newbury Park, CA: Sage.

Morgan, D. (Ed.). (1993). *Successful focus groups.* Newbury Park, CA: Sage.

Rubin, H. J., & Rubin, I. S. (1995). *Qualitative interviewing: The art of hearing data.* Thousand Oaks, CA: Sage.

Stewart, D., & Shamdasani, P. (1990). *Focus groups: Theory and practice.* Newbury Park, CA: Sage.

PART 4

Personal Development and the ■ Role of the Researcher Cycle

Selected Exercises ■

O chestnut tree, great rooted blossomer,
Are you the leaf, the blossom, or the bole?
O body swayed to music, o brightening glance,
How can we know the dancer from the dance?

W. B. Yeats

The exercises in this section are exercises I have adapted for allowing learners to develop techniques in interpretation. Modern dance, as an art form, is characterized by a language of movement; no two speakers of the language make quite the same statement in dance. Likewise, the dancer explores new ways of moving that include creative experiences and interpretation. In my usual work with mostly graduate students in education and human services, who have spent many years in bureaucratic settings, these are the exercises that create the most disequilibrium. At the same time, they offer the practitioner the most opportunity for self-awareness. In fact, many individuals come to the realization that qualitative methods are much too demanding for them, and they would prefer to work in the other paradigm. This in itself is, of course, a creative awakening. Just as everyone in dance must end up asking the question, "Do I really want to be a dancer?" the prospective qualitative researcher must ask the question, "Do I want to be a qualitative researcher?" Nonetheless, as a teacher, I see these exercises as a beginning point for self-identification and consequently as valuable for any researcher. For the prospective qualitative researcher, these exercises help to instill an awareness of the *importance of the role of the researcher.* I require potential qualitative researchers to be able to describe and explain their own role in their individual projects. We begin with a seemingly simple exercise, again modified from my days as a student of drawing. The exercises in this section are framed within John Dewey's notion of the aesthetic as part of everyday experience. In Dewey's time, there was a prevailing modernistic dualism that separated the aesthetic from the world of ordinary experience. In this post-modern time, I have constructed these exercises to help the individual address the dualism and engage in ordinary experience as aesthetic experience.

Exercise 1 ■

Writing Your Name ■

Purpose:	To write your name as many times and in as many ways as possible on an 8 1/2 × 11 paper. Use any design and placement for all the names you use. (Some examples appear in Figures 4.1 and 4.2.)
Problem:	To liberate yourself from the usual writing of your name
Time:	Take as much time as needed.
Activity:	Create a visual representation of one's own name.
Aim:	The purpose here is to give the person the opportunity to break away from the typical expression of writing one's name. This is so personal an exercise and produces such confusion for some because it is a first experience of creativity in a long time. I also see this as the

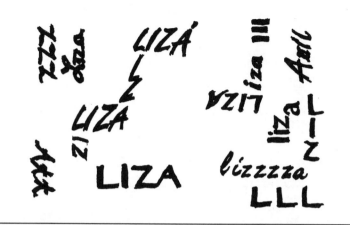

Figure 4.1. Name Writing, Sample Prepared by Valerie Janesick

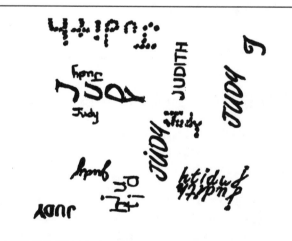

Figure 4.2. Name Writing, Sample Prepared by Judith Gouwens, 1995

beginning step, a first step, in recognizing the active nature of the role of the researcher. The researcher is not passive. Prospective researchers must begin to be able to recognize their own investment in the research project and how critical the definition of their role in the project remains.

Discussion: 1. How did you approach this exercise?
2. What was most difficult for you?
3. What have you learned from this?

Evaluation: Continue working on self-evaluation for your portfolio.

Exercise 2 ■

Photography Exercise ■

In the second exercise, the learner progresses from the internal to the external arena by using a camera to document a familiar social setting.

Purpose: In 1 hour, use a roll of film to take photographs of any area of campus or your workplace.

Problem: To document some portions of a familiar setting

Materials: Individuals need a 35mm camera and a roll of film. Those who do not have a camera need to purchase a disposable camera, now available in many places for under $10.

Activity: Shoot a roll of film to document as many different aspects of the environment as possible. Select your five best photographs to share with the group for next week. If working outside the class situation, find someone to discuss your work.

Of all the exercises I use with learners, this one seems to inspire the most confidence, awareness of one's limitations, and the most enthusiasm for finding out what kind of qualitative researcher one might become.

Evaluation: Continue on self-evaluation for your portfolio.

Exercise 3 ■

Building a Collage: My Role as a Researcher ■

Purpose: To design and construct a collage that represents your own role as a researcher in the project you are developing for study.

Problem: To capture your perspective on your role as accurately as possible.

Time: 2 to 3 weeks

Activity: Construct a collage on poster board that is a manageable size for display and discussion in class. Suggested size, 24 × 36 inches. Use any media you wish: printed text, photographs, magazine ads, newspaper headlines, objects, and so on.

Discussion:

1. How did you approach this activity?
2. What issues and ideas about your role as a researcher are emerging as you construct your collage?
3. What was the most challenging part of the activity for you?

Evaluation: Continue on your self-evaluation and overall evaluation for your portfolio.

Rationale: Students who select this activity become actively involved in representing their own feelings and ideas about their role as a researcher.

Exercise 4 ■

Constructing a YaYa Box ■

Purpose: To design and construct a YaYa Box. This is adapted from the field of art therapy. A YaYa box is a box designed to represent a person's innermost self on the inside of the box and the person's outward self on the outside of the box.

Problem: To capture yourself as you are now in terms of your current role in your research project.

Time: Take as many weeks to develop, create, and construct this with the presentation of the box at our last class meeting.

Activity: Find a box of any manageable size, from the size of a cigar box to a steamer trunk size. Use multimedia to build your box. The inside of the box will depict your innermost feelings, thoughts, and beliefs about who you are as you participate in your research project. The outside of the box will represent your outer self, or how your participants see you. Use any objects, text, decorations, and so on, to convey your idea of your role as the researcher.

In less than two pages to accompany the finished artwork, describe the contents, decorations, and meaning of your YaYa box.

Discussion:
1. How did you approach this project?
2. What issues about the role of the researcher confronted you as you began and implemented this project?
3. What was the most difficult part of this activity for you?

Evaluation: Continue with self-evaluation and overall evaluation for your portfolio.

Rationale: Individuals become intensely absorbed with this activity and focus on deconstructing their own role in the research project. The ability of learners to go deeply into reflection on their role and its effect on the research project is evident. Figures 4.3 and 4.4 are two sample descriptions of a YaYa box.

Description:

My YaYa Box is a metal candy box about the size of a small shoe box. The outside of the box is covered with a dark blue wool material to represent my outward appearance of being formal or reserved. On the center of the top, is a photograph of my immediate family, symbolizing their importance as the center of my life. Around the sides of the box are several miniature toys (reluctantly contributed by my two boys), which are hot-glued to the box. These miniatures portray various things that occupy my time. There is a car, a bicycle, a house, a computer, a school bus, and a miniature book.

Contents:

There are 10 items inside the box (*see attached packing list*). These items serve to motivate and encourage me as I struggle toward my Ph.D. Some items, such as a miniature version of my master's degree, remind me of my past. There is a letter from my 6-year-old nephew asking me if I am an English teacher (*yet*). A book jacket from John Steinbeck's *The Grapes of Wrath* (an example of ethnographic research) reminds me of my qualitative research project in education. A wrist watch reminds me that time to get my doctoral degree is running out. A "happy face" trinket reminds me to keep on smiling.

    The outside of my YaYa box is permanent. It is glued, and set, and not likely to change. The contents on the inside of my box, however, are not permanent. I intend to take out some of these items as time goes by and replace them with new contents as my educational, career, and personal interests change.

Packing List[a]

Contents	Purpose
1. Diploma, Master of Science in Education:	I did it once, I can do it again.
2. Master Army Aviator Wings:	To remind me of my first career
3. Letter from my nephew:	To encourage me to reach my goal of being an English teacher
4. Book jacket (*The Grapes of Wrath*):	By John Steinbeck
5. Cassette tape (Janis Joplin):	"You can't burn the candle at both ends"
6. Watch:	"Time . . . marches on"
7. Happy face:	Keep on smiling
8. Package of vegetable seeds:	Keep a hobby (gardening)
9. Snow White and the Seven Dwarfs:	Shift my favorite dwarf from Dopey to Doc (positive identity change)
10. Photo of my family:	To keep my priorities in line

Figure 4.3. Description of a YaYa Box by Dennis Dolan

a. Every effort has been made to ensure that your YaYa box has been properly packed. However, should you find an error, please call our toll-free number (1-800-980-YAYA) and we will promptly mail the appropriate item.

I call this YaYa box "what you see is what you get" because it resembles my life, dreams, beliefs, and feelings of the past, present, and future. I created it from scratch. Everything you see was hand-made, except for the bride and groom dolls and the pins, which reflect my love for arts and crafts. I built the box myself out of Plexiglas, which is a material that reflects how I view myself. Like Plexiglas, I believe I'm a very open person and I have nothing to hide. In addition, the material is tough but is easily scratched, which is very much the way I am: secure and consistent in my work relations, but my feelings can be easily hurt and scratched. This box has three portions in it.

Part 1

The crashed plane represents my shattered dream to become a pilot, which had a great influence on my life. The desk, books, and certificates resemble my academic life. The three green certificates stand for my elementary, junior high, and high school education. The red ribbons represent my stressful years earning a bachelor's degree and master's degree. The desk portion represents the past and present, and me always at the desk studying with a bit of a mess around, rather disorganized, but focused nonetheless. The prayer rug signifies my faith as a Muslim. The heart in the middle of this section stands for my married life, where the bride and groom are standing, and is the center of my attention, even while I am completing my Ph.D.

Part 2

This portion represents my state of mind today, especially after completing my ministudy for this class. During my observations as I studied the Lawrence Islamic Center, many questions began to haunt me about my own academic purposes and my future career. In fact, I actually feel that my mind is in a blackout these days. That is why I chose black for the background, but the question marks are in white, because I am optimistic about my future. Because my academic dreams depend on getting my Ph.D., I made a white certificate rolled up and tied with a red ribbon to symbolize my eventual completion of the degree.

Part 3

This part of the box represents my future dreams of establishing a home at home in Saudi Arabia after completing my studies here. The architecture of the house model is very much what you might see in Saudi Arabia. The green dome on top of it resembles the Prophet Mohammed's tomb (peace be upon him) in Madinahh, which is my hometown as well. The blue and green around the house is my wish to lead a comfortable and relaxed life there. The plants symbolize my wish for achievements, whether academic, personal, or spiritual and where children, research, and teaching will be the center of my life.

Figure 4.4. Description of a YaYa Box by Ahmed Zafir

Exercise 5 ∎

Journal Dialogue with Persons, Works, ∎ *the Body, Society, and Major Life Events*

Introduction: In working with prospective qualitative researchers, one of my goals is to inspire my students to keep a journal. They read the text, *At a Journal Workshop: Writing to Access the Power of the Unconscious and Evoke Creative Ability,* by Ira Progoff (1992). This text offers an extremely sophisticated and challenging approach to deepening one's self-awareness. On my view and Progoff's view, deepening self-awareness helps to sharpen one's reflection, writing, thinking, and ability to communicate. Thus, for the qualitative researcher, the meditative focus of journal writing can only help to refine the researcher as research instrument. The ideal situation would be to work through every component of the text, which I see as a lifelong task. Because we are time-bound in our class by only 16 weeks together, I have adapted some of Progoff's ideas into a workable routine for my students and myself. Progoff writes about journalizing as a Life History Log. The following framework is adapted to make the student a better researcher, with apologies, of course, to Ira Progoff.

Purpose: To keep a journal in dialogue form over the length of the semester. Set aside a minimum of 15 minutes each day for writing.

Problem: The individual records minidialogues with the self in the present, focusing on:

1. *Persons*
   Focus on a dialogue with key people in one's own life: best friends, lovers, partners. What have you discovered about the person you are today as a result of these dialogues?

2. *Work/Projects*
   Focus on a dialogue about significant projects or work that takes up a great deal of your energy. Which projects succeeded? Which failed? What have you discovered about yourself as a result of these projects?

3. *The Body*
   Focus on your own view of your own body. How have you cared for

it? How do you treat it today? Are there moments in your life history when you mistreated your body? What have you discovered about yourself as a result of awareness of the body?

4. *Society*
   Focus on your relationship to social groups. What groups are you a member of? How do you describe your own ethnic and racial identity? Are you aware of your political beliefs? Are you reconsidering how you relate to groups? What have you discovered about yourself as a result of awareness of your relationship to society?

5. *Major Life Event(s)*
   Focus on one or more life events that had a profound effect on the person you are today. What have you discovered from reflecting on this?

For many learners, keeping a journal is a new experience and by reading about journal writing, and by doing a journal as an activity, learners begin to reflect more deeply on their role as a researcher and as a human being.

Exercise 6 ■

Haiku and the Role of the Researcher ■

Purpose: To write a haiku about the role of the researcher

Problem: To capture the essence of the individual's role in the particular ministudy undertaken during the semester

Activity: The student is introduced to haiku, 17-syllable Japanese poetry in its classic form, 5-7-5, or five syllables in line one, seven in line two, and five in line three. Also introduced is the 14-17 syllable form. *Haiku is the poetic form most like qualitative work because it takes its imagery from careful observations.*
     Many complain that they are unable to write poetry, so I give them some of my own samples of haiku, as well as other students' work.

Amazingly, they seem to feel exhilarated after seeing that they are indeed able to do this. Figure 4.5 includes some samples of my own haiku upon completing various components of my long-term studies.

Exercise 7 ■

Framed Photograph Exercise ■

Purpose: Describe a framed photograph of a familiar person. Then pair up with someone, exchange photographs, and describe the other person's selected framed photograph.

Problem: 1. Individuals think about and use time to describe the framed photograph they themselves bring to class.
2. Next they pair off and exchange their own framed photograph with their partner. After receiving their partner's photograph, they each describe their partner's photograph.
3. Partners stop to share/discuss their descriptions. Each group of two has two descriptions to review and find differences and similarities. This is designed to prepare learners for analysis of data exercises later.

Time: At least 15 minutes for each of the two descriptions; in total, at least 30 minutes of time for description and equal or greater time for discussion.

Activity: This activity serves to sharpen awareness of the role of the researcher by working with a familiar artifact, a framed photograph of someone dear to them. At the same time, it extends and reviews observation expertise by moving to the description of an unfamiliar photograph. By pairing off, learners have the opportunity to practice communicating with another researcher about something in common, which is how to approach both descriptions and how to compare and contrast descriptions. This is a precursor to the next round of exercise, which includes practice in interviewing individuals and analyzing interview data.

Although strictly speaking this forces the individual to observe, and could fit in the observation cycle of exercises, this exercise allows for a transition to interviewing and analysis of data and focuses on discovery of the role of the researcher.

Discussion: Following the exercise, individuals are asked as a group to respond to the following questions:
1. How did you approach the first part of the activity? The second part?
2. What differences did you find in your own thinking as you approached each description?
3. What was the most challenging part of the exercise for you?
4. Volunteers are asked to read samples of their descriptions.

Rationale: This exercise again is part of the practice of disciplined inquiry designed to make the researcher more reflective. Reflection on the actual mechanics of approaching the description of the photographs is the first part of the activity. Second, individuals are forced to reflect on their own role as a researcher. By discussing this with another person, members see similarities and differences as part of the scope of disciplined inquiry.

■ Summary of Part 4: Personal Development and the Role of the Researcher

Due to the fact that the researcher is the research instrument in qualitative research projects, these seven exercises have been designed to sharpen awareness of the role of the researcher. This can be traced to the 17th-century text *The Mustard Seed Garden Manual of Painting,* which was part of a larger work, *The Tao of Painting.* Nearly everything written by the Chinese master painters was aimed not just at the technique of painting but at the painter's spiritual resources in order to express the spirit, or Chi, the breath of Tao. The Chi is looked upon as an underlying harmony. Likewise in dance, the spirit of the dance must merge as part

Haiku Samples

Field notes, Tape recorder
Dreams and Stories,
Who am I today?

Migrant study, 1984

Inner Silence
Writing, Reflecting, Hoping,
Slipping into Truth.

Migrant Study, 1985

Your story, my story,
Our story,
Pulls me into peacefulness.

Deaf Culture Study, 1986

Interviewing moments,
Take me by Surprise,
Like sunlight.

Deaf Culture Study, 1988

Willingness to fail,
Easing into silence,
Stumbling upon secrets.

Deaf Culture Study, 1989

Seeing past happening,
Hearing between Words,
Touching Heart Stories.

Judith Gouwens, 1995 Principal's Study

Figure 4.5. Role of the Researcher

of movement. These exercises are akin to the Chi meaning of painting and the spirit of the dancer's movement. To stretch, the qualitative researcher must be able to articulate the role of the researcher as the underlying harmony or spirit of the study. The qualitative researcher is always dealing with lived experience and must be awake *to* that experience and *for* that experience. By acknowledging and articulating the complexity of the role of the researcher, we are now able to begin the next cycle of exercises in this series, the Analysis Cycle.

■ Work Cited in This Chapter

Progoff, I. (1992). *At a journal workshop: Writing to access the power of the unconscious and invoke creative ability.* Los Angeles: Jeremy Tarcher.

■ Supplemental Readings

Berg, B. L. (1995). *Qualitative research methods for the social sciences* (2nd ed.). Boston: Allyn & Bacon.

Edwards, B. (1979). *Drawing on the right side of the brain.* Los Angeles: J. P. Tarcher.

Von Oech, R. (1986). *A kick in the seat of the pants.* New York: Harper & Row.

Wujec, T. (1995). *Five star mind.* New York: Doubleday.

PART 5

The Analysis Cycle: Intuition, ■ Ethics, and Other Issues

Writing permits me to be more than I am. Writing permits me
to experience life as any number of strange creations.

Alice Walker

Returning to the dance metaphor, if these exercises represent the stretching in a dance class, analysis of data and interpretation of data represent the floor exercises and performance stages of dance. After completing the series of exercises in observation, interviews, and the role of the researcher, learners have stretched a bit. They had a taste of some aspects of analysis of data through study of interview transcripts and fieldnotes. Working either alone or in groups, learners practiced developing categories from the data, looking for points of tension and conflict, and in general, focusing on making sense of the data. As Wolcott (1995) pointed out there is a difference between analysis and interpretation. In order for prospective researchers to realize their interpretation skills, it is important to think about the use of intuition in research just as it is used in choreography.

The role of the qualitative researcher in research projects, much like a historian's role, is often determined by the researcher's stance and intent. Likewise, choreographers create dances with knowledge of where they fit in the history of dance. In addition, both the dancer/choreographer's and the researcher's role is one where all senses are used to understand the context of the phenomenon under study, the people who are participants in the study and their beliefs and behaviors, and of course, the researcher's own orientation and purposes. Still further, it is like the ending in an O. Henry story. In other words, it is complicated, filled with surprises, open to serendipity, and often leads to something unanticipated in the original design of the research project. At the same time, the researcher works within the frame of a disciplined plan of inquiry, adhering to the high standards of qualitative inquiry, and looks for ways to complement and extend the description and explanation of the project through multiple methods of research, providing that this is done for a specific reason and makes sense. Qualitative researchers do not accept the misconception that more methods mean a better or richer analysis. Rather, the rationale for using selected methods is what counts. The qualitative researcher wants to tell a story in the best possible configuration.

■ The Qualitative Researcher as Historian

The qualitative researcher is most like a historian in that special access to sources is critical. When appropriate in research projects, the qualitative researcher relies on many possible sources of data and uses a variety of methods in the process, including but not limited to observation, participant observation, interviews, documents, the researcher's personal reflections, and so on. From the conceptualization of the research project to its completion, the researcher needs to be direct in terms of identifying biases, ideology, stance, and intent. It is usually the case that the qualitative researcher wants to understand the situation under study and must decide if the stance is taken from the inside or outside, as participant or observer or some combination and to varying degrees of both, and whether or not the researcher will approach the project holistically or not. Like the historian, the qualitative researcher must choose a point of view either as an apologist for what occurs or as the intimate insider, standing back looking at the whole and explaining each part of the puzzle. These are the crucial questions that need to be dealt with before entering the field. It is wise to pilot-test observations, interviews, and any type of participant observation that is being considered for the research plan. By doing a pilot study of limited duration, one is able to get a taste for the setting, become acquainted with personnel, and test one's skills as observer and interviewer. Just like a historian then, the qualitative researcher uses primary sources either as an insider and participant or as an outsider. As participant, one has the advantage in terms of special access to sources. As a role model, we might look to Thucydides, who did his own writing and data collecting, for example. More recently, we might look to the great historian Allan Nevins, who pioneered oral history methods and constantly demonstrated the importance of the insider's view of the social setting and its participants.

■ The Qualitative Researcher as User of All Senses Including the Intuitive Sense

One of the amazing strengths of the qualitative researcher, as I have written previously (Janesick, 1994), is the ability to use all the senses to undertake the research act. Sight, hearing, touch, smell, and taste often must be used to collect data. After living in the field with participants over time, the researcher also uses intuition, informed hunches if you prefer, to plan the mode of inquiry, to undertake the inquiry, and to develop a way of "seeing" what is evident in the social setting. The role of the qualitative researcher, much like the artist/dancer's role, demands total involvement and commitment in a way that requires a total immersion of the senses in the experience. As Dewey advises, art is the bridge between experience of individuals and the community. So, too, the qualitative researcher is someone who must establish a bridge as a part of the community under study. The qualitative researcher takes on the implicit task of working in a given community and does not have the luxury of being distant, apart from the experience under study, or "objective." I only wish to point out that the role of the qualitative researcher is a role that embraces subjectivity in the sense that the researcher is aware of the researcher's own self, in tune with his or her own senses, and is fully conscious of what is taking place in the research project. Subjectivity is something to be acknowledged and understood. Without understanding where one is situated in the research act, it is impossible to claim consciousness and impossible to interpret one's data fully. Meaning is constructed in the ongoing social relationship between the researcher and the participants in the study. It is no longer an option to research and run. The researcher is connected to the participants in a most profound way, and that is how trust is established, which in turn allows for greater access to sources and which ensures an involvement on the part of participants that enables them to tell their respective stories. Those who have conducted long-term qualitative studies know that participants in the study want their voices to be heard and do not want to be abandoned after the research project. In my field, education, there is a long history of researchers who come into a school, collect data, and flee. Thankfully, this is changing in terms of researchers' sensitivity to maintaining contact and a relationship with participants in the study, to maintain the sense of community that is part of any qualitative research project. This relationship remains as part of the research context throughout a significant period of time well beyond the end of data collection.

As I mentioned earlier, the senses are used in an intelligent way. Although sight and sound are obvious senses employed in doing observations and interviews, the other senses may be used while conducting research at various sites. For example, the researcher may need to interview a participant at a restaurant or coffee shop. Once while interviewing a participant in a blind and deaf research project, I had to sign into the person's hand, thus using touch in a way I had never used it before. Beyond this, however, all researchers use a sixth sense, an intuitive sense, to follow through on hunches that emerge from observing and interviewing in a particular social context. Researchers ought to have the opportunity in their training and in practice to sharpen their intuitive skills, which often opens up avenues of data previously unknown or hidden. In exercises I give my students to become better listeners and better observers, I often see the prospective researcher refine some of those intuitive skills so needed in research and life.

■ The Qualitative Researcher and the O. Henry Virus

Metaphorically speaking, and using literature as a point of study, I like to think of the O. Henry twist on life as a virus that each of us as qualitative researchers carries within us; in the proper setting and context, the virus becomes full blown. For those who have not delighted in O. Henry's work, a great deal can be learned from this superb writer, also known as William Sydney Porter, a master of description and one of the great observers of the human condition in all its frailty and silliness. All of O. Henry's stories describe people, places, and events from everyday life and celebrate the ironies, contradictions, and twists of fate that circumscribe anyone's life. I think of O. Henry as the quintessential model for the qualitative researcher because O. Henry endings are filled with surprises and make perfect sense, given the story. So, too, the qualitative researcher often stumbles onto something in the course of a research project that leads to a rich course of inquiry and that was unplanned in the original design of the study. In other words, one builds in a type of latent flexibility that enables the researcher to find, through serendipity, a tremendous amount of meaningful data for a fuller picture of the study. To use just one example, in a recently completed 8-year study of successful deaf adults, I interviewed one of my sign language tutors, who was from Canada. In a chance moment, she mentioned that she was going to meet some other international students and asked me to come along. By doing so, I met three more individuals who wanted to take part in the study and who in their respective interviews opened up new facets of deaf culture to me. One of the deaf students was friends with her interpreter, who was a child of deaf adults, which then opened up to me the part of the deaf community made up of CODA members, Children of Deaf Adults. By meeting and interviewing these participants, I came to a fuller and more meaningful understanding of what it means to be deaf with a capital D, deaf of deaf parents, versus deaf of hearing parents.

Back to the O. Henry virus and its meaning here. The qualitative researcher should expect to uncover some information through informed hunches, intuition, and serendipitous occurrences, which in turn will lead to a richer and more powerful explanation of the setting, context, and participants in any given study. The qualitative researcher is in touch with all of his or her senses, including the intuitive sense, or informed hunches based on key incidents and data from the research project. Furthermore, the qualitative researcher may expect the unexpected, as the writer O. Henry demonstrates in his short stories. The O. Henry virus, metaphorically speaking, is a virus that qualitative researchers carry and that becomes full-blown under a particular set of circumstances in a given social setting, and with key participants who allow for amazing twists and turns in everyday life. For the qualitative researcher, the role becomes expanded in that the number of options for coming upon new data is enlarged, for one can always count on serendipity, contradictions, and surprises in everyday life, the true domain of the qualitative researcher. Furthermore, the qualitative researcher describes and explains these occurrences as part of the discussion of the research process and or the researcher's role.

As when the dancer moves across the floor with floor exercises, analyzing data involves the researcher actually *doing* the work. For the research in progress, the researcher sifts through mounds of data; looks for emerging themes, ideas, issues, conflict, and tension; and checks back with participants to verify the accuracy of these points in the journey. After the researcher has sifted through the data transcripts, fieldnotes, and other documents, the good analyst uses the following guide to move on to reporting and interpreting data.

■ Checkpoints for Data Analysis, Reporting, and Interpretation

1. Look for empirical assertions supported by the data.
2. Use narrative vignettes and exact quotations of participants to support your assertions.
3. Scan all other reports, documents, letters, journal entries, demographic data, and the like; use direct references.
4. Include interpretive commentary related to the data, for data simply do not speak for themselves.
5. Include a theoretical discussion and relate your data to the theory that guided the study and give a hint to your readers of what will be included in your model of what occurred in the study.

6. Be sure to include a thorough description of your role as the researcher as part of the analysis and the history of the inquiry.
7. State clearly any and all ethical issues that arose in the study.

These checkpoints make it possible for your readers to experience the study, its social context and setting, and the range of evidence used to support your assertions, and to view the work in progress throughout the entire history of the inquiry. In addition, the range of ethical issues encountered in a study should be part of the analysis and interpretation of a study.

■ Ethics and the Qualitative Researcher

If the qualitative researcher can be assured of serendipity and contradictions, another area of assured study is that of ethics. In conversations about works in progress, dissertations, class projects, and the like, learners need a forum for discussing those ethical issues that arise in any given field setting. To prepare for discussing these everyday moments of fieldwork, learners have an opportunity to discuss and react to actual cases of ethical dilemmas previous students have encountered. To warm up the group in discussing ethical issues, learners assemble in groups and choose one of the following actual cases for discussion. Think of these two exercises as stretching your thinking about ethics and fieldwork.

■ True Stories: Sample Ethical Dilemmas

■ Discussion Exercises

1. "Just Delete That Data"

Recently, a doctoral student was conducting interviews on tape for a study that was designed to describe and explain the quality of a federally funded music and arts camp for the handicapped, with a particular focus on teacher effectiveness. The seven teachers were teaching music, art, piano, voice, and composition. The student conducted interviews with all the teachers over a 6-month period and observed in the seven classrooms. He also transcribed all the tapes and found that one teacher was totally neglecting his work as an instructor. Not only that, all the other instructors knew that one of their group was doing this, was basically unqualified, as well as being rude to students and arbitrary in assessment of students. The researcher showed this data to the director at a member check discussion. The director was also one of the teachers. In the discussion, the director revealed that he hired that teacher and could not accept the results of student evaluations or the comments from other instructors. The teacher in question was an old friend. Furthermore, the director asked the researcher to delete all comments referring to that teacher in case the data would jeopardize funding for the next summer.

2. "I Never Said That"

A doctoral student was interviewing female administrators, over a 2-year period, about their perspectives on their roles as women in administration. All interviews were taped. One of the female high-level administrators, in the course of the interview, disclosed that as a child she was abused by her father, who was an alcoholic, and that she decided not to have children lest she inflict anything on them that she once experienced. Later, when the researcher met with this administrator to conduct a member check and discuss the write-up of the case study, the administrator said, "I never said that." The researcher very tactfully pointed out that she had said that and that it was on tape. Once again, the administrator denied this and threatened to drop out of the study if the researcher even hinted at this in the case study write-up.

■ Questions for Discussion of Both Cases

1. How would you handle this?
2. What is the role of the researcher in this case?
3. What ethical issues are raised in this case?
4. What would you change, if anything, in this situation?

◼ Summary

Of course, there are endless examples of ethical questions in qualitative research studies. These two cases are here to offer some examples for discussion. Actual examples each semester provide grist for the forum, and by using group members to share viewpoints, prospective researchers at least begin to grapple with ethical issues and write a description of these issues in their reports. Likewise, doctoral students need to write about and include ethical questions that arose in the study as part of the ongoing explication of all components of qualitative work. In dissertations, writers often include the ethical questions in the methodology section under "Role of the Researcher" or in the Appendices as needed and depending on the nature of the ethical issue.

◼ Rules of Thumb for Qualitative Researchers

Throughout my experience, whether at public presentations of this material or in the classroom setting, a number of questions regularly arise and as a way of responding to those questions, I have written earlier (Janesick, 1990) of rules of thumb that guide our work and respond to these questions. As you look at these rules of thumb, you will easily identify the question that resulted in this heuristic tool.

1. Try to Refrain From Studying Your Own Group

Researchers for many years have warned against this. In class, students who have studied their own group have found the difficulties and anguish far greater than any benefits. As a member of a group, you may be too close to that group to be fair and accurate in your reporting.

2. Always Have an Outside Reader

As you may know, Malinowski, Powdermaker, Mead, Bateson, and other classic anthropologists used outside readers of their fieldnotes. Novelists and playwrights also use outside readers to bring a fresh viewpoint, to read for discrepancies, and the like. Especially as a researcher in training, it is wise to use an outside reader of your fieldnotes and interview transcripts. Other writers (Lincoln & Guba, 1985) suggest the use of an audit trail from the field of business. This is a fine idea if one has the time and extra money for such. However, as one who relies on the arts and humanities for my history and being, I prefer the use of the outside reader because it offers a long and dependable history in our field.

3. Design Your Study to Understand

Qualitative work demands that the researcher avoid trying to prove something. Instead, the heart of our work is understanding the social setting and all that it entails.

4. Time in the Field Equals Time in Analysis

I have always agreed with those who hold to this guideline. If you spend a year in collecting data, expect to spend a year in analytic time. The large amount of text to pore through demands a thorough and just accounting of the data.

5. Develop a Model of What Occurred in Your Study

In qualitative work, theory is grounded from the data, the words of your participants, and your fieldnotes, transcripts, and other written records. By developing a model of what occurred, the reader of the report is more able to make sense of the data and follow the researcher's argument. This also takes the report to another analytical level.

6. Always Allow Participants Access to Your Data

As qualitative researchers, we have an obligation to our participants to allow easy access to fieldnotes, journals on the research project, interview transcripts, and initial and final categories of analysis. In fact, this should be built into the informed consent document.

7. Look for Points of Conflict, Tension, and Contradiction

Looking for what does not make sense in a study, what doesn't quite fit, and in fact what exposes points of conflict often yields amazing information and insight. As the researcher goes through mounds of data, points of conflict offer a good grasp of events and are fruitful points of departure for analysis and interpretation.

8. Estimate Your Time and Costs

Inevitably, new qualitative researchers are amazed at the cost of transcriptions, duplication of sections of the report or dissertation, as well as the cost of supplies and equipment. Estimate about $2,000 for completing a long-term qualitative study for the dissertation. Currently, transcribers are charging about $75 for transcribing 1-hour tapes. Some researchers negotiate with a transcriber for the cost of the total package. Tape recorders, tapes, video recorders, and so on can be purchased used or new at reasonable prices; for example, a used video recorder is about $500. Likewise, time is your most precious and valuable commodity. Whatever your target date for completion of a study, add 6 months for a reasonable window of reflection and rewriting.

These guidelines are not meant to be all-inclusive, but they do respond to some of the most often asked questions about the nuts and bolts of doing qualitative research projects.

■ Attributes of the Qualitative Researcher

Many beginning qualitative researchers often remark about the difficulty of doing a qualitative research project. They are often amazed at the significant and in-depth time and energy commitment required to complete and sustain the project. Consequently, a forum is needed to discuss with a reflective posture exactly the qualities needed to complete such a project. Over the past 20 years, students have engaged with me in such discussions, and so we offer this list of qualities that may be helpful for new researchers.

■ Attributes Needed to Conduct and Complete the Project

1. A high tolerance for ambiguity
2. A strong determination to complete the study fully
3. A willingness to change plans and directions as needed
4. Resourcefulness and patience
5. Compassion, passion, and integrity
6. Willingness to commit to time in the field and equal time in analysis
7. Ability to trust and question others
8. Ability to know oneself
9. Authenticity
10. Above-average writing ability

Although this list is not meant to be exhaustive, these qualities emerge in nearly every discussion of this nature. In fact the last point, above-average writing ability, is critical in terms of representing data, analysis of such, and interpretation of the data. The qualitative researcher must be an excellent writer.

■ Writing as a Pedagogical and Research Practice

The reader may remember that fieldnote writing, journal writing, and doing descriptive vignettes in general have been part of the exercises described in this text. I have always been struck by the power and place of writing in my career as an educator. In fact, as I wrote (Janesick, 1995) earlier, most of my life consists of writing, reading other people's writing, editing, and rewriting and evaluating the writing of myself or others. What is ironic to me is that in research programs of doctoral students, so little emphasis is placed on writing as a pedagogical tool and writing as a preeminent focus of research dissemination. In my classes in research, students often express amazement at the amount of reading and writing required to be a good researcher, yet months or years later, they express gratitude for having that opportunity to realize writing is a chief component of qualitative research.

Furthermore, writing accompanied by reflection on that writing often leads to new questions about the research act, the study being reported, and questions in general about society, social justice, and responsibility. When learners reflect on this, within the framework of their research, they often remark on a feeling of empowerment. When individuals keep a journal of their own thoughts on the research process, create an interactive journal with the participants in the study, or write letters to me or other researchers, they discover and articulate their own theories about their research practices. What results is a kind of active learning from one another so that power is decentered and the research process is demystified. In addition, writing is one of the acts of democratization of the research process. Writing engages, educates, and inspires, which can only be helpful in trying to understand what qualitative researchers do in their respective research projects.

■ Interpretation

Interpreting the data after a presentation of major and minor categories of the findings is a chief responsibility of the researcher. Because qualitative work relies on grounding the theory in the data, researchers usually develop a model of what occurred in the study. This model may be represented in visual terms with drawings and graphs or in verbal terms. Look at the model of a study by Judith Gouwens (1995). She studied two principals in the City of Chicago Schools and was interested in describing and explaining their personal reality in terms of what kind of leaders they were. Her variables that affected the two principals' personal reality were

1. The nature, range, and variety of experience of each principal
2. The social interaction dimension of these experiences
3. The emotional response to these experiences
4. Reflexivity and meaning seeking of the individuals

With these four categories, Gouwens compared and contrasted the two cases relying on this model from the data in the study.

This is just one example of how interpretation of data can be rendered. The point is that each researcher must interpret the data for the reader. It is the final act of the researcher in any given project. In addition, the researcher needs to be aware that readers of the research may make entirely different meaning from the data and use it in a way that may even be at odds with the researcher's own interpretation. This is one of the hazards of research in general; yet, the researcher's responsibility to complete a study includes interpretation of the data, whatever it may be used for at a later date.

■ Summary

Analysis and interpretation of the data in any given research project must include a clear description of unintended moments in the research, intuitive informed hunches, ethical concerns and issues, and a serious description of the researcher's role in the entire history of the project. Analysis of data is very much like the dancer's floor exercises. Floor exercises follow stretching exercises in dance warmups. After floor exercises. the dancer's next step is performance of a given dance. Interpretation of data by the researcher is like the dancer's act of performance. It can occur only after long-term practice and work. The normal checks and balances in qualitative research work include a reasonable long-term commitment to the research practice at hand, relying on a stability embedded in a long-term activity. Likewise, the study of dance relies on stretching and floor exercises before moving into the realm of performance. The exercises described in this book rely heavily on the arts and humanities for their inspiration. Observation exercises, interview exercises, role of the researcher exercises, writing exercises, evaluation exercises, and discussion of ethical issues exercises all provide an opportunity for learners to stretch. These exercises were designed to allow one to stretch from one point to another in a focused pattern of practice to educate and inspire individuals so as to become better qualitative researchers. By using activities from the arts, such as drawing, photography, and dramatic art, individuals may discover new ways of thinking and opening the mind. By relentless writing activities, such as journal writing, description of beliefs and behaviors, letter writing, and self-evaluation, learners widen their repertoire of research skills. Likewise, physical and mental construction of collages, YaYa boxes, wreaths, posters, and so on also expand our notions of how we can become sharper at research skills in the field by sharpening our senses. The researcher is the research instrument in qualitative research and must be ready to become physically sharper at observation and interview skills. This is like the dancer, who relies on the body, which is the instrument with which the story of the dance is told. As Martha Graham put it so well, "the body is the instrument through which life is lived and which tells the story of the dance" (DeMille, 1991). For those of us who pursue qualitative research questions and design qualitative research studies, I hope that these exercises provide one way to approach developing a stronger body and mind for completing qualitative research projects.

■ Works Cited in This Chapter

DeMille, A. (1991). *Martha: The life and work of Martha Graham.* New York: Vintage.

Gouwens, J. A. (1995). Leadership for urban school change: An interview observation study of personal reality of two Chicago elementary principals. Unpublished doctoral dissertation, University of Kansas.

Janesick, V. J. (1990). Bilingual multicultural education and the deaf: Issues and possibilities. *The Journal of Issues of Language Minority Students, 7.*

Janesick, V. J. (1994). The dance of qualitative research design: Metaphor, methodolatry, and meaning. In N. K. Denzin & Y. S. Lincoln (Eds.), *Handbook of qualitative research* (pp. 209-219). Thousand Oaks, CA: Sage.

Janesick, V. J. (1995). Passion plays: Letters, diaries, narrative, and music as pedagogy. *The Review of Education, Pedagogy, and Cultural Studies, 17*(3), 289-296.

Lincoln, Y. S., & Guba, E. G. (1985). *Naturalistic inquiry.* Beverly Hills, CA: Sage.

Wolcott, H. F. (1995). *The art of fieldwork.* Walnut Creek, CA: AltaMira Press.

Appendix A ■

1. Can you describe how you first became aware of your deafness?

2. How do you see yourself today, in terms of your deafness?

3. What does your deafness mean to you?

4. Can you describe any particularly difficult or traumatic experiences in your life related to your deafness?

5. Can you describe how you fit into deaf culture?

6. To what extent do you consider yourself active in both the deaf world and the hearing world?

7. What, if anything, would you change about yourself if you could?

8. How does your family view your deafness?

Appendix B ■

Nonparticipant Observation—Fieldnotes ■

■ **Kim Zier (excerpts)**

Kim Zier, 1-23-95
Patrons, Asst. Mgr.
Oak Park Mall Fun Factory

7:25-8:00 pm I did a floor plan. I
focused on the mall, the store,
design of the video arcade
machine. I took notes and decided
not to polish them. Then I entered
the Fun Factory at 8:00pm.

The Asst. Manager, AM, asked me
what I was doing. I told him I was
a student doing research. "sounds
interesting, have fun" I told him I
selected the machines, Virtual
Fighter 2, and Virtual 1 Instinct to
observe. I told him I didn't want a
hot (busy) machine and I would
leave if he needed me to do so.
Told him I was a teacher and
wanted to watch who played the
games. Most patrons were around
high school age, all male, At one
point a female entered with a male.

I decided to watch a non busy
machine to ease into this. I finished
the floor plan. I will return
tomorrow. I told my wife about the
AM questions, She said he
probably thought I was a pervert,
which I had not thought of.

Appendix C ■

Sample Floor Plan ■

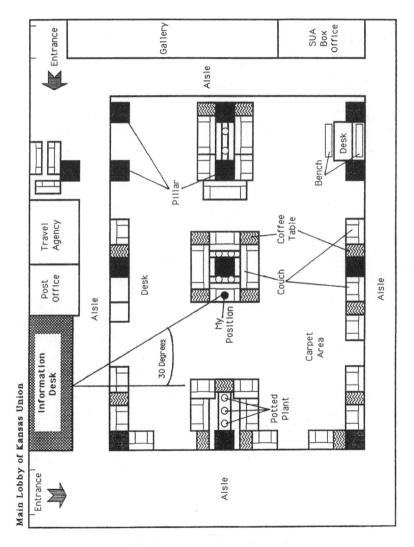

SOURCE: Created by Chin-kuei Cheng, 1994; used with permission

Appendix D ■

Sample Journal Entry ■

■ A Journal of My Research Process
Beth Easter (selected excerpts)

March 1, 1996

Today was my second day "in the field." I was much more relaxed today than I was on Tuesday. It may also be that I feel more comfortable because I was observing and trying to get a physical description of this office today. In comparison to the nonparticipant observation study, I feel less strange about sitting here and observing. I wonder if the participants feel comfortable about this.

I find myself thinking of the description of this area and the activity going on in terms of Tuesday's interview. I also notice I have difficulty describing people. I seem to want to describe the Action more than anything else. Is this because of personal bias? or the purpose of the study?

My most recent experience here at the university has been in academics, I was a letterwinner in undergrad school in field hockey. I have coached for 15 years and have always been a fan of athletics. Perhaps this will add greater depth to and understanding of my analysis and interpretation of the data? I understand the language of athletics. I might have someone look at this data for a triangulation of readers. (the outside reader as a check and balance of this system)

March 6, 1996

I was glad to have my laptop today. It makes any chair a workspace and saves me time in entering fieldnotes into the word processor.

I find it difficult to organize my observation today. Perhaps it is because I am trying to observe the people in the office today rather than the layout of the rooms and the space. I wrote a description of the Asst. AD following my interview with him on Tuesday.

I was drawn today to the flow of people in the office and the work each person is doing. This makes sense given my purpose of the study to look at the organizational culture of the department.

Appendix E ■

Student Journal in the Field ■

■ Peter Gitau

March 1st:

Today is the beginning of my field observation. I am feeling very excited for this is the first time I go into the field to study race relations at this university. I am thinking this is such a large community (over 20,000 students) and I am not sure how I will begin. I talked to my wife about it and she wished me well. Another thing I have been battling with is how to think about my own experiences as a black person.

March 2nd:

It is Saturday. I am just moving around the campus and already I look for details about race relations here. I am just finding it so hard to find blacks. They seem so few here on campus. Or maybe I am looking in all the wrong places. I will give myself more time to see what happens.

March 5th:

I am so excited because something unexpected happened. A white girl in my Swahili class introduced the subject of race out of nowhere. She asked me in front of class whether I have been discriminated against because of my skin color. This resulted in a lively discussion in class and I was able to get many perspectives from the class members. Most said that it does not really matter at all. And one of the students agreed to be interviewed by me for my study! Wow!

I visit the union. A group of students is playing rap music. There is only one black guy in the group and he is the vocalist. I look around and I am the only black person in the audience. I am trying to figure out why the audience members are here? The vocalist tries to crack a joke but nobody laughs. I am still trying to observe black students. The few I see are always in a group.

Appendix F ■

Self-Evaluation From a Former Student ■

■ David Smith

You ask what I learned from doing this study. This is about people, Valerie. If academics can do research by taking people out of it, it's no wonder that I never enjoyed reading about "research." By doing these interviews and observations I learned more than I ever dreamed was possible. People told me things I was not expecting on the one hand and yet I totally believed in their trust and faith in me. Especially when doing this research on gay and lesbian teachers, I was very deeply touched and moved that my teachers would open up so much to me. They knew I was an activist for gay and lesbian rights but I don't think that was an issue. I think it's people to people trust. They were authentic and honest with me in all their stories because I took the time to ask them—and to listen to them.

I think I learned that I was changed in this process as well. I myself was always doing more and more as a teacher to prove that I was as good or better than the next guy—the straight guy. I am not surprised by my major findings that gay and lesbian teachers do more than the average teacher—yearbook, photo club, debate, coaching, whatever—teach more classes! I did this myself at one time and I guess I am getting a doctorate to prove to myself I am as good as the next person. I also learned that you have to be a top-notch writer to do this kind of research. Of course you must be an exceptional writer to capture the stories of your teachers just as they want it told (their story). I know I have improved in terms of my writing but that's not enough for me. I want to teach people about human rights and this study inspired me to do this very thing.

Appendix G ■

Summative Evaluation Sample—Self-Report ■

■ **The Power of Transformative Agency**
Patricia Williams Boyd

Because of the rich layering of contextual information and artifact at work in any given site, this class has given me dynamic tools. This was a multilensed camera so to speak through which conceptual, theoretical, and practical issues about fieldwork were addressed. The class challenged me to go beyond the obvious and to present my data about other people's lives in holistic terms and those which push critical consciousness.

Because I work with disenfranchised populations, power is a concern of my work. I came to a keener awareness of uses and misuses of power through this course. Qualitative inquiry recognizes the power of the individual voice. It inverts the relationship between researcher and researched. Both are intertwined in the project. Qualitative Inquiry is driven by an insistent curiosity about people, the human condition, and all its layers of meaning. My aim is not only to create new knowledge but to improve the human condition. This is a liberatory pedagogy which goes beyond the ordinary.

Appendix H ■

Qualitative Research Methods—A Sample Syllabus ■

■ Instructor: Valerie J. Janesick

[This is my basic outline for my course. It is only inserted here as a sample for those interested in what a course might look like. I change the texts every other term to keep up with the latest new offerings that will assist learners.]

This course will focus on major issues, theoretical bases, and forms of qualitative methods of inquiry. Students will broaden their repertoire of inquiry skills by practicing qualitative methods, including participant observation and interview techniques. Students will conduct a ministudy and analyze interview, observational, and historical data sets. Each student will show competence in one of the following forms of inquiry: philosophical, ethnographic, narrative, aesthetic, historical, or action inquiry or any other alternative approach. Students will read major texts and current articles and discuss problems generic to fieldwork, including ethical and practical problems. Finally, students will become familiar with the use of microcomputers in qualitative methods of inquiry.

Theme:

> Some set great value on method, while others pride themselves on dispensing with method. To be without method is deplorable, but to depend on method entirely is worse. You must first learn to observe the rules faithfully; afterward, modify them according to your intelligence and capacity. The end of all method is to seem to have no method.
>
> *Lu Ch'ai*
> *From: The Tao of Painting, 1701*

Purpose: This course will provide experience in the investigation of a research question in a social setting. Students will practice interview and participant observation techniques and will analyze and interpret data collected. All students will discuss their work in progress and problems generic to fieldwork. Readings and class topics will include the following: Formation of research questions, access and entry into field settings, ethical questions in fieldwork, design of noncoercive inquiry strategies, qualitative analysis of evidence, descriptive validity, and theory building. Fieldwork will be supervised and may form the basis for future dissertation work or publications. This course will encourage the student to appreciate and understand the role of the qualitative researcher in terms of understanding the kinds of questions suited to qualitative research. Ethical issues in qualitative studies will be addressed.

What this course intends to accomplish: This course is designed to:

1. Introduce graduate students to the major concepts, issues, and techniques of qualitative research.
2. Develop in students a familiarity with the major writers and sources presently and historically influencing the development of qualitative research in education.
3. Present the philosophical underpinnings of qualitative research, specifically, phenomenology.
4. Enable the students to understand what kinds of methods are useful for discovering certain kinds of information.
5. Enable students to read, write, reflect upon, and discuss key issues in field research methods; to practice observation and interview skills; and to experience analysis skills by analyzing data sets from in class activities.
6. Help students plan and conduct a field-based research project using ethnographic research methods, specifically, participant observation, interview, and document analysis. Enable students to use video and audio equipment and transcription equipment.

Methods of instruction: Include but are not limited to small-group discussion work; Socratic method of questioning students; large-group discussion; reading, writing, and reflecting; guest speakers on occasion; minilectures as needed; hands-on activities with observations and interviews; analysis of taped interviews in small groups and in pairs.

Required reading: These four texts are the backbone of your course this term. You are encouraged to read more, of course.

Altrichter, H., Posch, P., & Somekh, B. (1993). *Teachers investigate their work: An introduction to the methods of action research*. New York: Routledge.

Berg, B. (1989). *Qualitative research methods in the social sciences* (2nd ed.). Boston: Allyn & Bacon.

Eisner, E. (1991). *The enlightened eye*. New York: Macmillan.

Maxwell, J. (1996). *Qualitative research design: An interactive approach*. Thousand Oaks, CA: Sage.

Recommended reading: For continued progress through the qualitative research cycle, select at least one of these books for reporting to the class. Each student must read at least one of these texts.

Creswell, J. (1994). *Research design: Qualitative and quantitative approaches*. Thousand Oaks, CA: Sage.

Denzin, N. K., & Lincoln, Y. S. (1994). *Handbook of qualitative research*. Thousand Oaks, CA: Sage. [*This will be on reserve at the library with a 2-hour limit. Selected chapters.*]

Lamphere, L., Stepick, A., & Grenier, G. (1994). *Newcomers in the workplace: Immigrants and the restructuring of the American economy*. Philadelphia: Temple University Press.

Miles, M., & Huberman, M. (1984). *Qualitative data analysis*. Beverly Hills, CA: Sage.

Mishler, E. (1986). *Research interviewing*. Cambridge, MA: Harvard University Press.

Morgan, D. (1988). *Focus groups as qualitative research*. Newbury Park, CA: Sage.

Progoff, I. (1989). *At a journal workshop*. Los Angeles: Jeremy Tarcher.

Rubin, H. J., & Rubin, I. S. (1995). *Qualitative interviewing: The art of hearing data*. Thousand Oaks, CA: Sage.

Short, E. (1990). *Forms of curriculum inquiry*. New York: SUNY Press.

Spradley, J. (1980). *Participant observation*. New York: Holt, Rinehart & Winston.

Van Manen, M. (1990). *Researching lived experience.* New York: SUNY Press.

Walsh, E. (1995). *Schoolmarms: Women in America's schools.* San Francisco: Caldo Gap.

Wolcott, H. (1994). *Transforming qualitative data.* Thousand Oaks, CA: Sage.

Wolcott, H. (1995). *The art of fieldwork.* Thousand Oaks, CA: Sage.

Yow, V. (1994). *Recording oral history.* Thousand Oaks, CA: Sage.

Earning extra credit: You may earn extra credit by reading any of the optional texts and as many as you choose and by writing a short 3- to 4-page reaction to the text. You will be given extra credit points to add to your average.

You may also earn extra credit by viewing a recent ethnographic film and writing a 3- to 4-page reaction to the film indicating the components of the film that relate to our class topics. Some examples of recent ethnographic films include *Schindler's List, Indochine, Farewell My Concubine, Ju Dou, Raise the Red Lantern, The Lover,* and *To Live.*

Research project requirement: Each student will conduct a field research project during the term. By the second class meeting, the student will identify the field site. The student will include descriptive demographic data, fieldnotes, interview data, and participant observation data in the field report. By the third class, students should be prepared to begin fieldwork during that week. At least 5 weeks of data collection are expected depending upon access and entry into the field site. Time in the field should equal time in analysis. The final report is due on the final class meeting date.

Assignments: There will be two major written assignments (graded):

1. A written synopsis of one of the texts from the Recommended reading list with the student's critique. The student will prepare a 3- to 5-page handout for class distribution and will present that information to the class.
2. A complete report of the field research project the student undertakes (20 to 100 pages).

There will be three minor assignments (S/U grading):

1. Nonparticipant observation/description assignment.
2. A sample of the student's category development from interview data.
3. The student's journal. Each student will keep a journal up to the point of leaving the field site. The journal should include thoughts, feelings, dreams, and any critical incidents associated with the research project.

OR

Rather than a journal, the student will design and construct a YaYa box. A YaYa box is a construction of the person's self. It is a technique used in art therapy but has been used in other fields. The box represents the person's inner and outer selves. The outside of the box is designed to represent the outer self. The inside of the box represents the person's innermost personality. It may be any size from the size of a shoe box to a trunk size. More on this later.

NOTE: Fieldnotes and interviews are part of in-class assignments.

Tests: There will be one midterm take-home exam.

Grading:
1. Students must inform the instructor *before* the due date if an assignment will be late.
2. Each project is worth a specific proportion of the final grade: [insert your proportions here]
3. Grading is based on the following scale: [insert your grading formula here]

The Handbook is a major text and will be discussed through-out the class because many of the chapters are relevant to your work in the field and connected to your other readings.

Class Calendar

Session	Topic	Preparation
1	Introduction to qualitative inquiry methods, Expectations of instructor; Non PO Assignment	Begin Berg
2	Case studies; process, methods, content, History, Foundations **Observation Activity #1**	Berg
3	Social context, interviewing **Observation Activity #2**	Berg
4	Generating research questions **Observation Activity #3** —First day in field	Eisner
5	Ethics of fieldwork, issues; Project updates **Interview Activity #1**	Eisner
6	Data collection—observational **Interview Activity #2** Method and fieldnotes	Continue Eisner and Handbook
7	Inferences and induction	Eisner, Maxwell
8	Data collection systems Interdisciplinary triangulation and intradisciplinary triangulation **Interviewing Part 3** in-class demonstrations	Student's choice In class
9	**Interviewing Part 4** Ethnographic analysis	Mishler; Rubin & Rubin Altrichter et al.; Wolcott
10	Objectivity and subjectivity; project updates	Begin Janesick chapter, complete Alt. Wolcott
11	Inference and proof in P.O. studies; handbook chapter as selected; project updates	Complete handbook chapters as assigned
12	Philosophical premises of qualitative research	Complete required reading
13	Ethical issues in fieldwork; historiography, life history Historiography, life history Oral history	Janesick chapter and Eisner Van Manen Yow
14	Interpretation of self-report data; understanding behavior in complex social settings	Complete choices
15	Critique of field research; Projects, Part I	All readings

Appendix I ■

Sample In-Class Handouts ■

■ **Terms Used to Identify Qualitative Work
(these are not meant to be all inclusive)**

Symbolic Interactionist Study
Ethnography
Life History
Oral History
Case Study
Participant Observer Study
Field Research
Naturalistic Research
Phenomenological Study
Descriptive Study
Ecological Study
Microethnography
Action Research
Narrative Research
Historiography
Literary Criticism
Interpretive Interactionist Study

Appendix J ■

Characteristics of Qualitative Design ■

Qualitative design is:

- **Holistic,** in order to understand the whole picture of the social context under study
- **Looks at relationships** within a system or subculture
- **Refers to the personal** face-to-face immediate interactions in a given setting
- **Focused on understanding the social setting** rather than prediction and control
- Demands **equal time in the field and in analysis**
- Incorporates a **complete description of the role of the researcher**
- Relies on the **researcher as research instrument**
- Incorporates **informed consent** documentation and is responsive to ethical concerns in the study

Appendix K ■

Questions Suited to Qualitative Inquiry ■

These are examples and not meant to be exhaustive.

1. Questions of the quality of a given innovation, program, or curriculum
2. Questions regarding meaning or interpretation
3. Questions related to sociolinguistic aspects of a setting
4. Questions related to the whole system, as in a classroom, school, school district, and so on
5. Questions regarding the political, economic, social aspects of schooling or any bureaucratic organization
6. Questions regarding the hidden curriculum
7. Questions pertaining to the social context of schooling, such as race, class, and gender issues
8. Questions pertaining to implicit theories about how the social world works in a classroom, school, hospital, family, and so on

Appendix L ■

Sample Miniprojects From Various Classes ■

This is a collection of topics from the qualitative methods classes that students undertook during any given semester. This is only a sampling of topics.

Peace on the Playground: A Study of a Quaker Preschool

Private Dancers: An Interview-Observation Study of an Exotic Dancer

An Interview Study of an ESL Teacher

A Case Study of a Juvenile Judge

Restrained Hope: An Interview Study of Chinese Citizens at Risk

A Study of Three White Males' Perspectives on Affirmative Action

Living on an Island: An Oral History of (name withheld) After the Berlin Wall

A Study of an Exemplary Principal

An Interview Study of Four Gay Teachers

A Study of a Local Tattoo Parlor and Its Patrons

A Study of the Lawrence Islamic Center

An Oral History of a Holocaust Survivor

The Other as Inmate: Perceptions of People in Prison

Appendix M ■

Sample Consent Forms ■

■ Exhibit A

I _____ agree to participate in this study

with _____. I realize no harm will come to me
and that this information will be used for educational purposes. I
understand I may withdraw from the study at any time.

Signed _____

Date _____

■ Exhibit B

[The researcher sends a form to the participants, which states:]

■ Affirmation of Intent

This is to say that I am conducting this study for educational
purposes, no harm will come to you and all information will be
treated with confidentiality and anonymity. You may withdraw at
any time and you will receive a copy of the full report. You may
see the data and anything I write at any time.

Signed _____
        (Researcher's signature)

Appendix N ■

Suggested Sections for the Qualitative Research Proposal ■

Due to the fact that I come from a tradition where the entire first three chapters of the dissertation are written as the proposal, I offer that here as the model practice. The value in this approach is obvious. Students have a familiarity with their literature and methodology and can clearly articulate their purposes and questions that guide the study.

■ Chapter 1: Introduction and Purpose

1. Introduction and background of the study
2. Statement of purpose of the study: The purpose of this study is to describe and explain a teacher's classroom perspective.
3. Exploratory questions that guide the study:
   a) What elements constitute this teacher's classroom perspective?
   b) What variables influence this perspective?

NOTE: The value of exploratory questions is clear. They provide the researcher with an open and wide opportunity for final analysis of the data and are to be included in the final chapter of results, analysis, and interpretation. The researcher responds to these questions, which are the framework for developing a model of what occurs in the study, all of which are provided in the final chapter.

4. Theoretical framework that guides the study: The theoretical framework that guides this study is Interpretive Interactionism.
5. Scope of the study
6. Outline of the remainder of the study and time line if applicable

■ Chapter 2: Review of Related Literature

1. Organization of this chapter
2. Historical background if applicable
3. Purposes of the review of related literature and how it relates to the purpose of your study and your exploratory questions
4. Acquaint the reader with your knowledge of the critical studies already published that relate to your study. You the researcher decide how many of these studies relate and what is the significant literature in your content area. You are the expert here. If you need to write about methodology literature, include it here.
5. Find the contradictions in the literature. Look for the themes and issues that directly relate to your purpose, questions, and research methods.
6. Find precedents in the literature for your work if possible.
7. If you are doing a historical study, it is possible that your literature review may be embedded in the purpose of the study and your design of this chapter may vary.
8. Work for an integrative review of your selected literature.
9. Look for recent work in the past 5 to 7 years, yet with an eye to the historical precedents of that work.
10. Summarize your review and connect this to the next chapter to introduce your methodology.

■ Chapter 3: Methods Used in This Study

1. Overview
2. Description of your methodology
3. Precisely state the rationale for your choice of methods.
4. Precisely describe the number of interviews, observations, supporting documents to be used.
5. Integrate your knowledge of the methodology literature here.
6. Describe your role as the researcher. Later, after data collection and analysis, go back and rewrite this section to accurately and precisely describe what it was that you did.
7. Describe and explain your pilot study.
8. Construct at least the first set of interview questions.
9. Provide the timeline for interviews, observations, and analysis of the data.

10. Provide the rationale for your choice of participants and describe informed consent. Include a signed statement from your participants agreeing to the study.
11. Describe your methodological assumptions and weaknesses.
12. Describe how you will collect and analyze data. Also describe any and all equipment used for data collection, for example, tape recorders, video recorders, photographic equipment, and so on.

NOTE: In qualitative studies, the researcher must disclose all pertinent information that applies to the rationale and conduct of the study. List all preconceived notions about this topic of your study. List all biases that apply. In this paradigm, researchers articulate their theoretical and practical beliefs. Be sure to tie your choice of methods to your purpose, exploratory questions, and literature.

Later, you will rewrite these first three chapters in the past tense, for the study will have been completed, and you may need to modify the original proposal. Remember, a proposal is a working document and not meant to be a slavish recipe. Also, while analysis is continual in the field, it is also after leaving the field that final analysis of data can proceed.

Your *fourth chapter* should be a *Presentation of the Data.* In qualitative work, it may take many forms, for example, as a narrative, as a series of case studies, as a dialogue, as a history, or as a reader's theater project. You the researcher must decide how best to present your data. Likewise, you may find the need to have more than the traditional five chapters of the dissertation, and that is entirely your choice. Be sure to have a rationale for that decision.

Finally, the *fifth chapter* should be a *Discussion of the Findings, Recommendations for Future Research and Interpretation of the Data.* This is where you the researcher have the opportunity to make sense of your study for the reader. Remember that the data do not speak for themselves. You must interpret the data for your reader. At that point, your responsibility as a researcher is complete. You do not have control of the study after that, for readers may make more or less of your data and in fact may render a completely different interpretation of the data. Your job is to be as persuasive as possible with the evidence to support your interpretation. This evidence comes from the words of your participants, taken directly from the interview transcripts and field observations. You must be precise in this final chapter, so that you bring the reader of your research to accept your explanations, conclusions, and recommendations.

After all this, you are ready to write the *Abstract* of your study, which is the abstract that all will read in *Dissertation Abstracts* worldwide. Be sure to include the purpose of the study, the questions that guide the study, the theoretical framework of the study, a description of data collection procedures, findings, and your major interpretive statements, all within the word limit.

Appendix O ■

Samples of Dissertation Proposals ■
With Focus on Methodology

In the following sections, you will find three samples of dissertation proposals using various qualitative techniques. Reference lists are not included.

■ **Sample 1**
An Outline of a Completed Dissertation Proposal
Using Interviews, Documents, and Observations

[This example displays the outline of the first three chapters of Dennis Dolan's dissertation.]

The Cultural Adjustment of International University
Students to American Academic Life: An Interview Study

Dennis Dolan
University of Kansas

Chapter 1: Introduction

Purpose of the Study
Exploratory Questions
Definition of Terms
Theory Base
Description of Setting
Summary

Chapter 2: Literature Related to the Study

Language
Cultural Adjustment

Academic Adjustment
Institutional Policies
Student Preparation
Summary

Chapter 3: Methodology

Role of the Researcher
Key Participants
Ethics
Data Collection
Data Presentation
Analysis and Interpretation of Data
Summary of Methodology

Purpose of the Study

The purpose of this study was to describe and explain the cultural adjustment process that international university students often experience.

Exploratory Questions

1. What elements constitute the cultural adjustment process of international students?
2. What variables contribute to the reduction of stress in the cultural adjustment process?
3. In what ways are international students prepared for their American academic experience?

Chapter 2: Literature Related to the Study

In this chapter, the author, Dennis Dolan, reviews the literature related to international students' adjustment to their new language, culture, and academic settings.

Chapter 3: Methodology

In this chapter, Dennis describes in detail the methods of his study.

■ Sample 2: A Proposal That Uses Focus Groups, Interviews, Artifacts, and Observations

[The following is an example of an edited proposal of a study by Marilyn Kaff. The major sections of Chapter 1 and 2 are condensed to let us focus on the complete text of Chapter 3, Methodology. The reader may find the completed dissertation in Dissertation Abstracts. It was completed at the University of Kansas in 1996.]

An Interview Observation Study of the Role of the Special Education Teacher in Inclusive Settings

Marilyn Kaff
Kansas State University

Introduction

Inclusive education is one of the most talked about issues in American education today. One cannot open a professional journal or watch a nationally broadcast news magazine without it being a topic of conversation. Both proponents and opponents want to have their say. Position statements regarding the efficacy of inclusion run the gamut from those who support full inclusion for all as a matter of principle (Stainback & Stainback, 1992; Thousand & Villa, 1990) to those who support inclusive school practices but express concern over implementation (Sailor, 1995; Vaughn & Schumm, 1995; Zigmond & Baker, 1995). There are those who seriously question the wisdom of inclusion for all students (Fuchs & Fuchs, 1994; Kaufman, 1993).

Educators are challenged by the rapid evolution of educational practices and services for students with disabilities. During the past 20 years, the proportion of students served in separate facilities and self-contained classrooms has declined, while the number of students with special needs served in general education is rapidly rising. A growing number of school districts educate almost all students in general classrooms, rather than in pull-out classrooms. At least 68.6% of students requiring special education services are served in the general education classrooms for part (40% or more) or all of the school day (U.S. Department of Education, 1991).

Purpose of the Study

The purpose of this study is to talk with and observe special educators who have had experience working in inclusive settings. I will describe and explain the personal reality of special educators who work in inclusive settings by looking at the attitudes, beliefs, and practices developed by special educators who have spent considerable time working inclusively.

Exploratory Questions

There are several questions that will guide the research: (a) What elements constitute the reality of inclusion for these special education teachers? (b) What are the variables that influence these elements? (c) What are special education teachers' beliefs and assumptions about the implementation of inclusion? (d) What are the skills and practices that special education teachers utilize in inclusive school settings?

Summary

This interview-observation study describes and explains the beliefs, skills, and practices of a group of special education teachers who work in inclusive schools. The exploratory questions that guide the study are: (a) What elements constitute the reality of inclusion for these special education teachers? (b) What are the variables that influence these elements? (c) What are special education teachers' beliefs and assumptions about the implementation of inclusion? (d) What are the skills and practices that special education teachers utilize in inclusive school settings?

This chapter introduces the study, provides a rationale, explains the interpretivist theory that will guide the study, and describes the purpose for the research. Chapter 2 reviews the literature on inclusion to provide a background for the study. Chapter 3 describes the role of the researcher in this study, the participants in the study, the interview-observation methodology to be utilized, and the form of the final report of the study. Chapter 4 will consist of the actual case studies of the special education teachers. Chapter 5 will present a cross-case comparison of the case studies along with findings and recommendations for further research.

[In Chapter 2, Marilyn reviewed the literature on inclusion, court cases related to inclusion and some of the arguments for and against inclusion. Now she was ready to go on to her methodology chapter.]

Chapter 3: Methodology

An interpretivist approach to the study of special education teachers is based on the assumption that there is not one reality of teaching, but many. Because reality is socially constructed, it follows it is also contextual in nature. Thus, inquiry into the role of special education teachers in inclusive settings must be qualitative. According to Janesick (1994), in qualitative research, the aim is to look for the meaning and perspectives of the participants in the study.

For teachers to delve more deeply into their practices, the use of narrative (that is to say teachers' stories) becomes important. With the advent of school reform, there has been a change in the role of the teacher. Teachers are no longer technicians; the teacher role has shifted to that of initiator of the curriculum and method. Connelly and Clandinin (1988) reported that much of teachers' knowledge about teaching comes from being a teacher. As teacher-researchers, many teachers begin to search their minds and hearts to examine their practices. Quite like a story, teachers as researchers do things, and as a result, situations change or things happen to people and as a cumulative result, people change their assumptions, practices, and skills.

Role of the researcher

According to Lincoln and Guba (1994), the role of the researcher in an interpretivist paradigm is that of a " 'passionate participant' actively engaged in facilitating the 'multivoice' reconstruction of his or her own construction as well as those of all other participants" (p. 115).

In this study, the aim of the researcher is to listen to and reconstruct the stories of the special education teachers as they interpret the realities of their role within the context of inclusive school settings. It is my belief that there are valuable lessons to learn through sustained study of those working in inclusive sites. For too long, researchers have ignored the expertise and knowledge of those working in the trenches; it is my aim to in some small way rectify this error. Through the use of qualitative techniques including narrative, focus groups, and participant observation, I hope to gain insight and knowledge from the workers in the field. It is my intent to provide a rich description of the way special education practitioners have transformed their work and the ways in which their practices will inform the knowledge base of the profession.

My background and beliefs

I must begin by setting forth my own agenda and biases. I have worked in the public school setting for the past 16 years. I have taught in special education for 8 years and regular education for 2 years, and I spent 3 years as a school psychologist. Most recently, I was a project coordinator for an elementary school that redesigned the service delivery system for students with special needs. The program made the transition from a resource/pull-out model to one in which all students were housed in the regular classroom. I have seen firsthand the struggles, frustration, and enthusiasm of teachers—both regular and special—as they try to cope with the changes and challenges of working inclusively.

Description of the participants

The key participants in this study will be 10 special educators who have worked in an inclusive school setting for at least 5 years. That is to say a setting in which most of the students with special needs are educated in the general education classroom. Recognizing that inclusive practices occur most frequently at the elementary level, the teachers who participated in the study worked in Grades K to 6. Furthermore, because changes in one's skills and practices evolve over time, the teachers need to have experience working collaboratively with regular education teachers.

The focus group facilitator will be Gwen Beegle. Gwen is a doctoral candidate in Special Education at the University of Kansas. Her role is to pose the questions, moderate the discussion, and ensure the quality of the conversation.

Data collection. According to Lincoln and Guba (1985), within the interpretivist domain, there are multiple constructed realities. To utilize these multiple realities, data for this study were gathered from multiple sources. This study utilized input from a focus group and interview-observations.

The focus group. The focus group is a relatively new addition to qualitative research methodology. Focus groups occupy a midpoint position between individual interviews and participant observation of groups. Focus groups allow researchers to observe the interactions of a group discussing a topic during a concentrated period of time. The group method is essentially a qualitative data-gathering technique that finds the interviewer directing the interaction and inquiry (Fontana & Frey, 1994).

The research began by utilizing a focus group. The purpose of the focus group was to identify issues around special educators working in inclusive schools. Participants were asked to reach consensus on a definition of inclusion. Additionally, they were asked to identify skills, beliefs, and practices they utilize in their everyday lives at school.

The design of the focus group interview. Like most focus groups (Morgan, 1988), the one for this study will use a moderator and will consist of a small group of 10 to 12 people. The participants in this group will be homogeneous with respect to the research question. They will be special education teachers who work in public school settings that are inclusive. The teachers selected will have worked in inclusive settings for at least 5 years. The topics for the focus group are contained in Appendix A [not included in this book].

Merton (1956) presented four criteria for a successful focus group. It should cover a maximum range of relevant topics, it should provide data that are as specific as possible, it should foster interaction that explores the participants' feelings in some depth, and it should take into account the personal context that participants use in generating their responses to the topic. These will be my guiding principles as I conduct and analyze the data generated by the focus group.

The focus group will be followed by in-depth interviews and observations with two of the participants. I will spend a number of days at each of the school sites. The skills, beliefs, and practices identified by the special education teachers in the group will become the focus for the follow-up observations and interviews.

Interviews

In-depth interviews of the two special educators will be conducted to reflect-on-action, which allows teachers to look back on their classroom practice (Schon, 1987). Narratives allow teachers to communicate about and reflect on their practice after it occurs. Through locating and relocating their voices within their own world of teaching, teachers gain insight into what they know, what they think, and who they are (Noddings, 1991).

These interviews will be generally unstructured; they will include descriptive questions to gather data about the special educators' perspectives on inclusion and structural questions to address the educators' perspectives on the relationships between the skills, beliefs, and practices they utilize in their everyday lives at school. The researcher will conduct 10 to 12 hours of interviews with each participant. These interviews will be transcribed so that a record of the data is established.

Observations

Spradley (1980) talked of three kinds of observations: descriptive observations, focused observations, and selective observations (p. 33). Data collection in this study was primarily descriptive. However, that is not to disallow the use of focused and selective observations. Descriptive observations will be conducted to generally describe the behavior of the special education teachers within the culture of the school. Focused and selective interviews will be aimed at specifically understanding the changing role of the special educator. These observations will include interaction of the special educator with general education staff, students, and groups of school and community personnel. The nature and the need of the focused and selective observations will be determined through analysis of the descriptive observations and data from interviews.

Artifacts

Artifacts in the form of documents from the teachers and the schools were also gathered. These documents include reports the school received from the state and the district, articles about the schools that have been published in the press, the special education teachers' own written communications, minutes from staff meetings, planning and grade-level team meetings, and so forth.

These multiple data sources, the focus group, observations, interviews, and artifacts provided a rich collection of data. They also allowed for data triangulation, which Patton (1990) described as a means of comparing and cross-checking the consistency of information derived at different times and by different means (p. 467).

Analysis of the Data

Data analysis in qualitative domain is an ongoing process that went hand-in-glove with the initial data collection. As the data are gathered, the researcher develops a system of coding and categorizing it. The researcher must find the most effective way to tell the story (Janesick, 1994). The analysis is ongoing, subject to constant vision and revision. As the patterns and themes are identified and supported through the data, they become categories for coding the data. Strauss and Corbin (1994) referred to this process as grounded theory. Once these categories are determined, relationships between the information within the categories are analyzed, and points of conflict are identified. Throughout the analysis, the input, reflections, and feedback of the key participants are sought to ensure the authenticity of the interpretation of the data. The narrative written from the analysis will consist of case studies (teacher stories) that describe each special education teacher's view of inclusive school practices. These narratives allow for a model to be developed from the comparison and contrast of the special educators.

Ensuring Quality and Credibility

Patton (1990) discussed three issues that must be addressed to ensure credibility in a qualitative study:

1. Rigorous techniques and methods for gathering high-quality data that are carefully analyzed, with attention to issues of validity, reliability, and triangulation
2. The credibility of the researcher, which is dependent on training, experience, track record, status, and presentation of self
3. Philosophical belief in the phenomenological paradigm—that is, a fundamental appreciation of naturalistic inquiry, qualitative methods, inductive analysis, and holistic thinking (p. 461)

A variety of strategies will be selected in the collection and analysis of the data to address these issues. To begin with, care is taken to gather adequate and appropriate data. Participants are asked to participate fully in the study. The focus group, the interviews, and observations are scheduled at the convenience of the special educators to ensure they had adequate time to reflect. The researcher will spend considerable time in the field to collect the needed data. The gathering of data through multiple sources allows for triangulation of the data. Outside readers will review fieldnotes and interview transcripts. The participants will provide input to and feedback on the narratives developed from the analysis of the data.

The researcher has had the training, experience, and antecedent knowledge to ensure credibility. The researcher took a variety of courses in research methodology, two of which were in qualitative research methods, during which she conducted a study of "agents of social change" and conducted a narrative oral history. To this particular study the researcher brought a wealth of antecedent knowledge of and experience in public schools and, more specifically, as an inclusion facilitator in several Kansas public schools. Finally, the researcher has a strong belief in the value of qualitative inquiry and narrative storytelling as a means of describing and explaining the role of the special educator in inclusive school settings.

Summary

This interview-observation study describes and explains the beliefs, skills, and practices of a group of special education teachers who work in inclusive schools. The exploratory questions that guided the study are: (a) What elements constitute the reality of inclusion for these special education teachers? (b) What are the variables that influence these elements? (c) What are special education teachers beliefs and assumptions about the implementation of inclusion? (d) What are the skills and practices that special education teachers utilize in inclusive school settings? Chapter 1 introduced the study and provided background and a theoretical basis for the study. Chapter 2 provided a review of the literature on inclusion in general, the impact of inclusion on general education teachers, and the impact of inclusion on special education teachers. This chapter described the interview-observation methodology that will be used to conduct the study. Subsequent chapters will include narratives of each special educator in the form of case studies and a cross-case analysis of the two.

Sample Interview Protocol

Initial Set of Interview Topics

1. Share your background in Special Education
2. Talk about inclusion—what is it? what are your thoughts about inclusion?
3. What are the elements that make inclusion work at your school?
4. What are the barriers to inclusion working at your school?
5. What are the skills that special education teachers need to work in inclusive school settings?
6. Describe a typical workday for you in your current setting.

Sample Letter to Participants

Dear _____:

I am a doctoral candidate in the School of Education at the University of Kansas. As a partial fulfillment of the doctoral requirements, I am planning to conduct a study of special educators who work in inclusive settings. The purpose of the study will be to describe and explain the role of the special education teacher in inclusive settings. Your participation in this study is requested because of your work over the past several years in a reformulated service delivery system for students with special needs.

Participating in the study will require approximately 2 hours of your time for the focus group and an additional 2 hours for an in-depth interview. The interviews will, with your permission, be taped and transcribed. To maintain confidentiality, you will not be identified by name on the tape. I will be transcribing the tapes. The transcriptions of the tape will be read by an outside reader; however, she will be able to identify the teachers only as teacher A, B, or C, etc. The tapes will be kept in a safe in my house. Each participant will be offered a copy of the tape as well as a copy of the transcription. The participants and I will be the only ones with access to the tapes. Once the tapes are transcribed, a master tape will be made from the originals and they will be erased. The master tape will remain in my possession.

A comparable amount of time will be required for conducting observations by shadowing you in a variety of situations related to your role in the inclusive setting. Interviews and observations will be arranged at the school at your convenience. Your name and the name of your school, and any other information gathered in this study, will remain confidential and will be used for educational purposes.

In the next week, I will be contacting you to answer any questions you might have concerning your participation in this study. At that time we can arrange a meeting to discuss the details of the interviews and observations for the study.

The focus group is tentatively scheduled for Thursday, January 11, 1995 from 6 to 8 in a meeting room at the Holidome in Topeka, Kansas. I appreciate your thoughtful consideration of my request. I look forward to your participation in the study.

Sincerely,

Marilyn Kaff
(addresses, phone, fax, email, etc.)

Sample Consent Form

I, _____ , have been informed about this study, and I agree to participate in this study with Marilyn Kaff. I realize that no harm will come to me and that the information will be used for educational purposes. I understand I am free to withdraw from the study at any point in time.

Signature _____

With my signature I acknowledge that I have received a copy of this consent form.

Dated _____Signature _____

■ **Sample 3: Example of a Dissertation Proposal Using Interviews, Observations, Photography, and Documents**

[This dissertation by Patricia Williams Boyd was completed in 1996 at the University of Kansas. The purpose of her study was to describe and explain, from the perspective of key participants, the concept of school-linked services, vis-à-vis full-service schools. The study took place in Modesto, California, at Hanshaw School. The literature reviewed included the literature on full-service schools, school-linked services, and their social implications. Here is the methodology chapter from the dissertation.]

A Case Study of a Full-Service School: A Transformational Dialectic of Empowerment, Collaboration, and Communitarianism

Patricia Williams Boyd
Eastern Michigan University

Methodology

Given the particular focus of full-service schools as the heightened extension of the school-linked services model, it is critical to select schools whose structure as well as philosophical perspectives reflects this paradigm. Although there are hundreds of schools across the country that are engaged in varying levels and degrees of service integration and collocation of services, there are fewer that are, given the aforementioned characteristics, actually full service. Hanshaw Middle School and its feeder school, Robertson Road Elementary, are full-service schools that have consented to be the subject of this proposed ethnographic, qualitative case study. This chapter presents the rationale for the methodology chosen as well as the elemental concerns with regard to conduct. Interview protocol, initial questionnaires, and constructed data analysis follow.

Because of the interpretive nature of qualitative research, it is important that the researcher's basic assumptions, upon which and through which the study is conducted, are explicated. This should facilitate the understanding not only of the choice of methodology but also of the positional analysis taken. And because this form of research reflects a critical tradition in that it will confront observed societal injustices, it is fundamental that the researcher's ideological imperatives and epistemological presuppositions are, at the inception of the study, articulated.

General Assumptions

1. With regard to data collection, behaviors will be described not measured; the sample will be intensive rather than extensive; and the data will result in the discovery of research questions.
2. Interpretation and meaning must be understood within the cultural context.
3. Truth cannot be constructed or understood outside of its social and cultural context.
4. The interpretation of truth does not exist apart from some set of ideological precepts.
5. There is no single voice or single truth that is dominant. Thus, this study assumes the research position of a postmodernist.
6. It is the process that is of most direct interest to this study, followed by the produce.
7. Reality is multiple, interrelated, and divergent (Janesick, 1985).
8. There are representative power relations at work within each institution as well as within the collaborative which are socially and historically constituted.
9. The power of language mediates the experience and the experienced against and within the subjective.

10. Research is, therefore, intentionally transformative and not intended only to record.

Specific Assumptions

1. There are disparate and dramatic inequities and inequalities in the general culture, which are reflected in the microculture of school.

2. The student-family must be viewed from an ecological perspective in order to gain the rich contextual meaning of the school-community.

3. The closer the collaborative project moves to an agency's perceived mission, the greater will be the agency's allocation of resources.

4. The more politically complex and socially disenfranchised a neighborhood, the more projects will be initiated within the full-service paradigm.

5. The greater the diversity of the school, coupled with the degree of professional and constituent insistence for assistance and change, the more pressure will be exerted to embrace a linked-service model.

6. Because schools service groups of people (regular or special education) rather than individuals, as social service agencies do, and are therefore not accustomed to operating in the community, they are the last to change in a linked-service collaborative (Hammiller, 1995).

7. Teachers have little formative professional training in collaborative, interdisciplinary areas, and principals, given the hierarchical structures of power coupled with the same lack of professional training, have even less.

8. The culture of the school as the culture of a community can be understood through direct, participatory observation and interview with the people of concern.

Assumptions of Belief

1. Contrary to the Marxist contention that they are capitalist agencies of social, economic, cultural, and bureaucratic reproduction, schools can be and must be sites of democratic possibility, resistance, and hope (Giroux, 1988), and they can and must be bastions of critical empowerment.

2. The potential success of a given school using the full-service model is directly related to the positional levels of experiential belief exercised by the participants.

3. Kids' performance (whether measurable in grades, attendance, participation, etc. or behavior and attitude) will improve as schools are made more relevant to the family by virtue of being experienced as a giving unit of care and concern.

4. When a family becomes directly invested in the workings of the school, e.g., decision making, service rendering, community embracing, its members will experience a greater relevancy of school to their daily lives and will feel school is not so removed from the reality of their lived experience. School will then assume a neighborhood-reflective and a "visional" culture, rather than a white, middle-class culture, and ownership will lead to more intrinsic attitudinal investments and achievements on the part of kids.

5. Neighborhood schools belong to the neighborhood. Those people who have historically been wrongfully and explicitly divorced by virtue of artificial school mandate, from their schools, are in fact the rightful owners.

6. All people want to better their lives; and all parents want their children to be successful, to have a part of the American dream.

Research Strategy

This study is seated in the arena of ethnographic inquiry, is based on grounded theory as understood from an inductive methodological perspective, and has gathered data from a single-case perspective, Modesto city schools.

Because of the rich layering of contextual information and artifact at work in any given site, ethnography describes and explains a given culture as it exists within a specified time (Janesick, 1991; Spradley, 1980). Ethnography investigates human behavior as it is understood and experienced within that particular subtext, given reality as it is created by the people of concern. Janesick (1991) fluently articulates the identity of ethnographic work to realize the larger picture or to present itself in holistic terms. It is the personal work of scrutinizing relationships within a given system or culture. It is work that is driven by an insistent curiosity in human definition and solution of problems. It is a work compelled to service the human need. Of the three types of ethnography—comprehensive, topic-oriented, and hypothesis-oriented—it is the latter with which this study is concerned.

The research strategy used in this study is also referred to as action research, which is built on grounded theory. Bogdan and Biklen (1992) define action research as the "systematic collection of information that is designed to bring about social change" (p. 223). Given one of the basic suppositions upon which this study is built, namely, that research should be transformative for the people of concern as well as for the researcher, action research captures the active role of the researcher directly involved in the cause for which the research is being conducted. Furthermore, as Short (1991) explicates, the self-reflective stance of action research addresses improvement in three areas: practice, understanding of practice by its practitioners, and the situation in which the practice occurs.

A strategy that offers a broader contextual understanding of the people of concern is called grounded theory. It is the development of theories grounded in empirical data of cultural description, well suited to the arena of ethnography (Spradley, 1980). Empirical evidence produces the actual theory, which is illustrated by characteristic examples of data, rather than using data to prove a priori assumptions.

Case study research is used to offer a framework that provides a detailed examination of one setting, a single depository of documents, and in this case, a single school district. In a case study, the major data-gathering technique is participant observation with the focus of study on a given organization (Bogdan & Biklen, 1992), in this case Hanshaw Middle and Robertson Road Schools. And although the group under study assumes a particular name, the study of the organization is intended in sociological terms to refer to the collection of people who share common expectations, therefore, expanding the people of concern to include the collaborative as it exists within and is a reflection of the community.

Also, common to the essence of case study work is the attempt to illuminate a decision or set of decisions: why they were taken, how they were implemented, and with what result (Yin, 1989). As a formal strategy for investigation and as a form of empirical inquiry, the researcher who employs the use of a case study:

- investigates a contemporary phenomenon within its real-life context; when
- the boundaries between phenomenon and context are not clearly evident; and in which
- multiple sources of evidence are used. (Yin, 1989, p. 23)

The desire to evaluate one school district and its attendant community, an unusual case representative of the conceptual model of full-service schools, positions itself well for the single-case study format.

Conduct of Study

Qualitative research is an interdisciplinary, transdisciplinary field that uses a multimethod approach to research. Its perspective is naturalistic and interpretive with regard to the understanding of human experience. It stresses the socially constructed nature of reality, the intimate relationship between the researcher and, what this writer calls the Mentor-Other—a positional view of those people who have been marginalized by the greater society and labeled as "other," but who are, in fact, the experts who guide the researcher through the area of study—and the situational constraints that shape inquiry (Denzin & Lincoln, 1994). It emphasizes the value-laden nature of inquiry and answers questions that stress how social experience is created and given meaning.

Through the inductive method of data analysis, thematic meaning emerges from within the context of the case, which is itself the extent of generalization. Also, inductive analysis begins with specific observations and at once unlayers the context under observation and layers the researcher's phenomenological understanding with general patterns. Categories emerge from open-ended observations as the researcher becomes more familiar with the empirical world of the people of concern (Patton, 1990).

The use of multiple data-gathering strategies underlies the case for qualitative research. This study uses participant observations, in-depth and elite interviewing, fieldnotes, an annotated log, detailed description using direct quotes and narrative vignettes, reflective accounts of participants, and visual data in the form of black and white as well as color images (photographs) to gather critical data in support of the written case record.

Participant observation. Whereas a participant comes to an event or situation only to engage in the activities, a participant observer comes to engage in activities appropriate to the situation and to observe the activities, people, and physical aspects of the situation (Spradley, 1980). Spradley continues to observe characteristics distinctive to the participant observer: She seeks to become explicitly aware of things usually blocked out, things that add significant information to the cultural setting; the participant observer is at once an insider and outsider within the social setting, thereby gathering data from both vantage points; and given the reflective charge of qualitative research, the participant observer must of necessity be introspective, constantly reassessing his or her own position, values, culture against that which is being studied. This type of immersion in the setting allows the researcher to begin to experience the Mentor-Others' reality as they see, hear, and live it.

In-depth interviews. Given that an interview is a method of data collection that may be seen as an interaction between the researcher and the Mentor-Other, the purpose of which is to obtain valid and reliable information, in-depth interviews are explorations that seek to discover general topics with regard to the subject, only as they emerge from the participant's meaning perspective (Marshall & Rothman, 1989). It is left to the Mentor-Other to shape and structure social phenomena with regard to the topic, as it unfolds in the natural setting, not as it is perceived by the researcher. It is of tantamount importance for the Mentor-Other to empirically understand the value of her/his expertise to the researcher, a phenomenon that will be addressed below.

To gain a wide-angle lens view, in-depth interviews were conducted with a family who volunteered to share both the historical perspective of the project as well as their own transformational experiences. Interviews were also scheduled with volunteer students, school faculty, neighborhood community organizers and leaders, a social worker, a case worker, and a mental health provider. Such interviews allowed the writer to triangulate findings across sources and against personnel interviews and to test issues of reliability and validity (Marshall & Rothman, 1989).

Elite interviews. Given varying levels of expertise, elite interviews were conducted with Hanshaw and Robertson Road Project leaders in each of the collaborative agencies. As well, in an effort to gain the perspective of those considered influential to the project, elite interviews were conducted with local agency leaders who assisted in the structuring of the project, its organizational structure, financing, and resource allocations.

Visual images. According to Ball and Smith (1992) the social organization of the visual experience is shaped by the notion that people's experience of the seen world is culturally shaped and socially constituted and mediated. Because the visual field encompasses more than the material world, abstract phenomena such as pain, protection, pride, anger, and other varied emotions may be captured. This writer was interested in how the people of concern ordered the experience of their own world as well as the participant-observer's sense of reality. Therefore, given this writer's long interest and history in photography, in addition to her visually recording the Hanshaw and Robertson Road Project via black and white film, disposable cameras were given to volunteer students in order to capture a comparative sense of community and ownership.

In addition to the above, and based on the necessity of gleaning multiple views of an organization (systems, human resources, political, and symbolic in nature), observations and interview schedules were established to gain insight from direct contact with a case management team in practice, a social worker in the process of home visiting, team meetings with the interagency collaborative, a presentation of a 3-year quantitative study of Robertson Road School by Stanford University, a site-team meeting, a newly established (as of 30 August, 1995) neighborhood block incentive team initiated by and consisting of parents, and a student organization directly responsible for responsive action within the collaborative as well as within the school. These interviews were tape recorded and transcribed by the researcher, the written analysis of which was offered to the project's leaders.

Research Interpretation and Presentation

The criterion for trustworthiness in qualitative research is not shaped or understood in the same fashion as in other traditional empirical designs. Validity in the qualitative paradigm is a text's call to authority and truth and as such is epistemological. A text's authority is established through recourse to a set of rules concerning knowledge and its production and representation (Lincoln & Denzin, 1994, p. 578). Therefore, alternative criteria were utilized in the establishment of trustworthiness. They were credibility, transferability, dependability, and confirmability.

Credibility. In addition to techniques such as prolonged engagement and persistent observation, one of the most fundamental criteria for establishing credibility is the triangulation of data. Triangulation of data confirmed the authenticity of the study's observations and subsequent findings, and it presented thematic presence against multiple perspectives.

Transferability. Because generalization is not the goal of qualitative study, external validity is understood in terms of transference, or the ability of the case study to describe a setting so others may use it as a source of comparison. It must be noted that validity to a critical postmodern researcher means far more than the positivist stance of internal and external. Internal validity to the qualitative researcher is a measure of the strength of truth of the study or the extent to which the researcher's observations were a true description of a given reality.

In addition, a third type of validity is imperative in the repertoire of the qualitative study, that being catalytic validity. By the above definition, action research must foster action on the part of the researcher as well as the respondent. It must move those studied to understand the world and the way it is shaped in order to transform it.

However, trustworthiness is more applicable to the qualitative study than any form of validity, the criteria for which are the credibility as witnessed in the portrayals of constructed reality and anticipatory accommodation, in which humans reshape cognitive structures to accommodate the unique aspects of what they perceive in the new contexts. Therefore, researchers learn from the comparisons of different contexts (Kincheloe & McLaren, 1994).

Dependability or reliability. Do the results presented truly represent the values, beliefs, and the norms of the participants? The people of concern were asked to review the written record of this study, in order to limit observer bias and to capture the essence of lived experience from the Mentor-Others' vantage point.

Confirmability. The conclusions drawn in this study were based on and supported by gathered data. Also, detailed information trails were maintained and evidenced in order to limit critique methods used during fieldwork.

The internal, ethical system that drives the narrative is based on new and emerging criteria according to Lincoln (1995). They are: fairness, ontological authenticity, educative, catalytic, and tactical. The limitations of the study must be discussed and presented openly. Truth must be understood as ongoing and fragmentedly carried through time, rather than as being staid or isolated. Lincoln concludes that the desired end of research is to serve the purpose of the community researched. Relational knowledge is grounded in community, and the power of liberatory action research lies in its ability to link with social action.

Reflexivity or subjectivity. Qualitative research also recognizes how power shapes our positionality, for the interpretation of reality is constructed against our own sense of the interpretive experience. As such the researcher must extend her or his consciousness, for the purpose of understanding subtle differences in others, to be critically self-reflective on both the macro level—the deep structural levels where contact points may collide with the personal—and on the micro or particular level, to be able to discuss contradictions in the narrative being presented, and to the end of transformative action.

Reciprocity. The method qualitative researchers use is one which clarifies the understanding of the people of concern as always existing in relation to the environment that embraces the researcher as one of such a community.

Voice. Most important, the qualitative researcher, according to Lincoln (1995), seeks out the silenced for their voices are often antihegemonic. The researcher becomes involved in changing the environment of the marginalized, a world of lived reality, laden with situation-specific meaning. The questions of to whom, by whom, and for whom give birth to an understanding of the complex world of lived experiences from the view of those who live it (Schwandt, 1994).

Research Analysis

Symbolic interactionism. According to Blumer (1969) an empirical science must respect the nature of the empirical world that is its object of study, and the methodological perspective that does so is symbolic interactionism. Through this view, meaning arises in the process of interaction between people; vis-à-vis, the "meaning of any given thing or event grows out of the ways in which other persons act toward the person with regard to the thing" (p. 4).

Therefore, meaning is seen as social products, as creations that are shaped in and through the defining activities of people as they interact, thus involving an interpretative process. Social interaction is then a process that forms human conduct rather than being a means or a setting for the expression of it (Blumer, 1969). And the understanding and construction of the self, critical to this paper, is the definition people create through interacting with others of whom they are one (Bogdan & Biklen, 1992). Such is this writer's interpretive position.

Ethnographic data. As has been explicated, ethnographic data analysis is a tool for discovering cultural meaning (Marshall & Rothman, 1989). Through the reflective accounts of participants, the researcher describes the empirical situation rather than studies variables. As such, the work becomes a cultural translation of symbols and the relationship between them; it becomes a relational transcription that seats others within their own cultural context. Fine (1994) maintains, "the project at hand is to unravel critically the blurred boundaries in our relation, in our texts, to understand the political work of the narrative" (p. 75).

Domain and taxonomic analysis. Spradley (1979) would offer domain and taxonomic analysis as other forms of understanding the data. Through domain analysis, relationships within the culture become a means of discovery of the domain parameters.

Taxonomic analysis includes the selection of a domain, the identification of a cultural frame, a shaping of subsets within the domain, and the construction and refinement of the engendered taxonomy.

Componential analysis. This form of analysis is a search for gaps within the data, for points of conflict, for the verification of previously analyzed data, and for emerging common thematic meaning within the symbols.

Furthermore, Denzin and Lincoln (1994) maintain that research analysis must be multimethod as it artfully interprets empirical data. Such also is this writer's position. The representational dilemma in the analysis process is one that challenges the researcher to question, "can I capture and recreate the power of lived experiences within this given social context?" In large part, this is done through the unlayering of cultural themes, the interpretation of relationships within the culture and their respective meanings, which paints a holistic portrait of the cultural setting.

It was only possible to draw authentic meaning from the complexity of human interactions, as evidenced within the communal purview of this study, given the power of qualitative analysis to see with a manifold perspective, to hear with an ear for both the silenced soloist and the cultural chorus both consonant and dissonant, and to interpret with a renaissance hunger for the world born in multiplicity, in interconnectedness, and in interpretive experience. It was only possible to both found and compound transformative meaning from a case study as presented herein, given the dynamics of qualitative research to empower the researcher with the tools of reflexive and reciprocated observation resonant in the lives of those this writer calls the Mentor-Others. And it was only possible to enjoin the spheres of dislocation, of passioned place, and of powered position portrayed by and exercised in the praxis of collaboration through the qualitative vantage of that which Modesto sought and understood as the common good.

Site Selection

As has been mentioned, Hanshaw Middle and Robertson Road Elementary Schools were selected for this study given their unique utilization of the full-service school model. Upon contact via telephone with the supervisor of the project, Patricia Logan, this writer's request was eagerly embraced, and a data-gathering procedure was immediately set in motion. Also, service provision for secondary kids is very different both in procedure and in perspective from that provided elementary students. Whereas comprehensive services for very young children has a long history of working with families of kids with multiple needs, as witnessed in a review of the literature and of current programs, there is often far less experience and/or commitment to the family-centered approach the older the kids become. Priorities change as the children age. And whereas the personalization of services is most important in the elementary years, by adolescence, confidentiality becomes an overriding concern (OERI, 1995). Given this paper's particular interest in the adolescent, and in disadvantaged populations, Hanshaw Middle School met the criteria for selection. Robertson Road Elementary School was also studied because the same Healthy Start personnel worked at both sites. Likewise Robertson Road, a feeder school to Hanshaw and an older established facility in a like-populated neighborhood, offered some comparative and ancillary understanding of what was in fact the Modesto Project.

Modesto is a northern California city of 175,000 whose socioeconomic foundation of traditional agriculture has evolved into modern agribusiness, the changing labor force reflecting a new ethnic mix. Chuck Vidal, the principal of a school to be built in a disadvantaged neighborhood, conducted a door-to-door survey of the neighborhood residents. Among all populations—poor Hispanics, recent immigrants from Cambodia and Laos, many families deficient in English—family ambitions were solidified in their hope for their kids to go to a school that would put them on the college track.

In 1991, building began on Hanshaw's new $13 million campus-like complex, featuring specialized facilities for music, arts and crafts, auditoriums, gymnasiums, and facilities for children with identified disabilities. The interdisciplinary curriculum features a team-teaching and cooperative-learning approach with kids. The college goals are reinforced by links to several campuses in the California State University system.

Hanshaw's primary focus, like that of other such school-linked services projects, was quality education. In 1992, legislation that called for partnerships among schools, social service organizations, and federal-state-local service delivery agencies, and called for others to provide supportive services to at-risk kids, was introduced; it was passed by Congress in 1993. Therefore, as student and community needs became clearer, social services were added to the already present school nurse, mental health clinician, and aides who assist immigrant populations. However, Hanshaw had no coordinated approach to providing full services until it secured two operational grants from California's Healthy Start program, which required a 25% match in funds by applicant localities. Then, with state grant and community resources, Hanshaw set a yearly budget of $400,000 across 3 years, concentrating resources on the center for health and dental care and an interagency case management team that linked students and families to a variety of social service agencies.

Researcher's Role

At the core of qualitative research is the commitment to the critical, transformative rigor that seats our perceptions of reality and of each other in the varied and shared stories of our citizenry. Researchers must be prepared to challenge all philosophical, historical, social, and contextual levels of understanding and of comfort and be prepared to shift the center of the world—both empirical and intellectual—from the dominant, Eurocentric tidiness of "we" and the "Other," to embrace a world, the essence of which is the difference of voice, of race, of ethnicity, of gender.

Although we are indeed ontologically separate beings, once the researcher-mentor relationship is entered, the presumptive position is one of supreme moral and ethical responsibility. It is the human spirit at its most triumphant, for it is the conquering of the moral being over what may be otherwise seen as the natural self. It is the striving to embrace the Other both as an extension of ourselves, yet as a separate and distinctly different being. In fact, we remove ourselves from the false sense of safety that conventional, dominant-culture wisdom provides and step outside the desensitized sterility that distance, presuppositions, and prejudiced generalizations offer. We release ourselves from the throes of purely predictable objective observation and common everyday social interaction, which exist in and see only the shadows, and we construct our being as a questioner, a researcher, a sojourner, a listener in the pursuit of the substance of the story told by the Mentor-Other.

Whereas our culture maintains social interaction based on a level of mistrust and on a measure of dishonesty in response to and in the formality of questions, we must presuppose complete honesty in the researcher-mentor relationship and rigorously seek only empathic, perceptive understanding. We must deliberately withdraw from the insulated and comfortable separateness that mere conversations perpetuate, and we must grapple with the guilt and the starkness that the mentor's story may well awaken within us, a story told and heard in collaboration.

The ethics of our conduct are the very practice of our moral principles and although our morality is neither decisive nor definitive, it does not occur as one stands alone and observes. It is rather the foundation for and the product of our interaction with differences, the intimate intercourse with the politics of the Mentor-Other. It is the narrative of mutuality and of contextual consensuality. Throughout the study, the researcher must be acutely aware of the continually shifting and tenuous Mentor-Other relationship, one grounded on equal dignity and mutual collaboration, one that returns voice to the silenced, one that empowers the disenfranchised to ownership and participation in the larger culture.

The researcher must be engaged in the discourse of change, of instability, of constant permutation as we deny our prescriptive places and rigorously do battle in the arena of cultural and social norms, of long-held rules that knowingly destabilize the Other in the service of justifying the self, of identities splattered with the mystified facades of disability, of disempowerment, and of denigration. The researcher must be an active voice in the discourse of manumission, the dialogical confrontation of power with self-realization, of the denial born of segregation with the borders bridged by empowerment.

When we as researchers come to the somewhat tenuous position of presenting the story, of interpreting the hours of fieldnotes, of supportive research, of intuitive pauses and painful gaps, we become the mouthpiece that speaks the mind of those who have been differenced out of the cultural dialogue. For those silenced by the ugly whispers of our own historical and social conscience, we bear an even greater burden to speak the unwanted, unheard, and unheeded truth as it screams its way across our newly emblazoned experience.

Our research, born of our own deconstruction, must stimulate a provocative insight to recreate a new, a more honest, a more inclusive social identity; for in the final analysis, we must exercise the conduct of our language in obeisance to all that is just and good in a world that is neither. In the experience of the people of concern, we learn to respect all that is irrational, unreasonable, unpredictable, and unjustifiable. We learn to have no less esteem for those on the fringes of society than we have compassion for the incongruity and disrepair of their stories. We learn to be moved by the disjointed and disjunctive struggles of those who could easily have been us.

What role do we play beyond that of researcher? In the reality of fieldwork, we cannot objectively remove ourselves from becoming involved in the lives of the participants. It is an involvement that often nakedly challenges us with the stark brutality of poverty, of basic want and unfulfilled need, of glaring absence in the land of presence, of cruel injustice and separation, of resentment, anger, and discontinuity born of powerlessness and hopelessness.

As researchers are we to affirm, to disavow, to act, or only to listen? Are we to speak to family members, to authorities, to other participants when confronted with critical information? Clearly, we are not therapists, medical doctors, philanthropic patrons to the poor, crusaders coming to right the wrongs of generations past and present. Yet, once we boldly step into the life of another, we do so not only as researchers, but as participants in and of the human experience.

It is ethically imperative for us to be translators who recount the stories told at the borders of our country's identity with the fervor that speaks of both the commonality of survival and of the fragmented quality of life, of dominant and subdominant, of the powerful and the powerless, of the intolerant and the tolerant, of the secure and of the angered, of the immoral and of the moral, of the complacent and of the empowered. And it is here that we speak of an empowerment of integration, of independence rather than dependence, emancipation rather than submission.

Appendix P ■

Guidelines for Mini Project ■

■ GUIDELINES FOR THE FINAL REPORT OF YOUR MINI PROJECT

What you need to include in the final report:

1. Title of the study which captures completely your study on a cover page, for example *Behind Bars: An Interview Study of a Bartender in New York*

2. An introduction to your study

   How did you select this topic? What makes you interested in this? Why?

   Explain and set the stage for your study

3. Purpose of the study

   The purpose of this study is to describe and explain _____

4. Exploratory questions which guide the study

   a. What elements constitute _____

   b. What variables influence _____

   (These are samples of broad open ended questions)

5. Description of the setting at all levels, description of participant/s

6. Description of a typical day in the life of _____

7. If you were to do a full blown study what literature might you review?

8. Description of the method you used in the study with quotations from our texts to support your choice of methods

9. Complete description of your role as the researcher

10. Select direct quotations from your participant/s which lead us to your main categories of what you found

    (This is your presentation of the data)

11. What did you find?

12. Develop a model of what you found. This may be depicted in a figure, tables, words etc. What did your data tell you?

13. Respond to your exploratory questions with data from your study to support your responses

14. Conclude something about the importance of your study for some audience

Index

Action research, 115
Analysis cycle, 2, 72
    checkpoints in, 64-65, 107
    inductive method in, 116
    intuition in interpretation, 59
    and qualitative researcher, 59-60
    research analysis, 121-122
Answer vs. question, pedagogy of, 6
Art as experience (Dewey), 7
Art of Fieldwork, The (Wolcott), 59
Art on my Mind (hooks), 3
At a Journal Workshop (Progoff), 53

Case study research, 115-116
Catalytic validity, 119
Checkpoints for analysis, reporting and
        interpretation, 64-65
Consent forms, 94, 111
Conversations. *See* Interviewing
Critical pedagogy, 6
Cunningham, Merce, 5

Dance as metaphor, 1-2, 4-5
Densin, Norman, 5
Description samples, 24f
Dewey, John, 7, 46
    Art as Experience, The Early Works, 7
Discovery of Grounded Theory, The (Glaser
        and Strauss), 5

Dissertation proposals, samples, 99-127
    focus groups, interviews, artifacts, and
        observations, 101-111
    interviews, documents, and
        observation, 99-100
    interviews, observation, photography,
        and documents, 111-127

Early Works, The (Dewey), 7
Educational Imagination, The (Eisner), 8
Eisner, Elliot, 5, 8
        *The Educational Imagination, The
        Enlightened Eye*, 8
Energy, economizing, xii
Enlightened Eye, The (Eisner), 8
Ethical issues, 65-67
Ethnographic Interview, The (Spradley), 30
Ethnography, 114, 121
Evaluation. *See* Self-evaluation
Experience
    and aesthetics, 46
    and art, 7
    as education, xiii

Fieldnote format, 15
Flax, Jane, 5
Focus groups
    approach to, 36-37
    defined, 34

history, 35
strengths/weaknesses of, 36, 37
uses of, 35
utilization checklist, 38-39
Freire, Paulo, 5

Gardner, Howard, *Multiple Intelligences*, 8
Giroux, Henry A., 5
Glaser, B. G. and A. L. Strauss, *The
Discovery of Grounded Theory*, 5
Grounded theory, 115
Gubrium, J. F., *Oldtimers and Alzheimer's*,
35

Habit. *See* Routine
hooks, bell, 5
Art on my Mind, 3
Horton, Myles, 5

Inquiry
and critical space, 2-3
cycles of, 2
fields of, 92
Internal/external validity, 119
Interpretation
checkpoints for, 64-65
of data, 59, 71-72
Interview cycle, 2
Interviewing
as conversation, xii-xiii, 29
defined, 30
focus groups, 34-39, 105-106
intuition and the senses in,
61-62, 64
preparation for, 31, 42
protocol, 75, 109
questions, types of, 30-31
Interviewing exercises, 32-42
analyzing data, 41-42
by telephone, 33-34
conclusions, 34
a familiar person, 32
focus group, 39-41
a stranger, 33
Intuition in analysis, 59, 61-62, 64

Journal writing. *See* Self-awareness exercises

Language of possibility, 6
Lincoln, Y. S. and E. G. Guba, *Naturalistic
Inquiry*, 68

Methods. *See* Qualitative research
Mishler, E.G., *Research Interviewing*, 30
Morgan, D., *Successful Focus Groups*, 39
Multiple Intelligences (Gardner), 8
Naturalistic Inquiry (Lincoln and Guba), 68

Nevins, Allan, 61

Objectivity, 61-62
Observation cycle, 2
Observation exercises, 14-25
an animal, 22
description samples, 24f
a familiar person, 20-21
in home or workplace, 19-20
as nonparticipant, 23-25, 76
physical description of setting, 18-19, 77f
self-evaluation, 17f, 18f, 26f
still life scene, 14-18
a stranger, 21-22
summative evaluation, 18f, 27
Observing. *See* Qualitative research
Oldtimers and Alzheimer's (Gubrium), 35

Pedagogy of answer vs. question, 6
Personal development. *See* Self-awareness
exercises
Phenomenology, 6
Porter, William Sydney (O. Henry), 63
Progoff, Ira, *At a Journal Workshop*, 53

Qualitative research
consent forms, 94
defined, 116
design, 1-2, 91
and focus groups, 34-39, 105-106
and knowledge, 6
methods, 4-5, 6, 10, 60-61, 84-89
model format, 27f
observing/reading, xi-xii, 14
participant observation, 117
points of inquiry, 92
and researcher, 56-57, 59-60
research proposal format, 95-98

social relationship in, 62
study projects, 93
syllabus sample, 84-89
terminology, 90
and trustworthiness, 107-108, 119-121
and wholeness, 7
See also Research process; Interviewing
Qualitative researcher
attributes of, 69-70
and ethical issues, 65-67
as historian, 60-61
and intuition and the senses, 61-62, 64
O. Henry as model, 63-64
rules of thumb, 67-69
and writing ability, 70-71
See also Role of researcher cycle
Qualitative studies, features of, 8

Reporting, checkpoints for, 64-65
Research Interviewing (Mishler), 30
Research process
focus groups, 34-39, 105-106
pedagogy of answer vs. question, 6
and theory, 5-7
See also Observation exercises;
    Interviewing exercises
Research proposal format, 95-98
Role of researcher cycle, 2, 46, 56-57
defined, 59-60, 103-104, 124-127
in research projects, 59-60

See also Self-awareness exercises
Routine, xii

Seeing, xi, 61
Self-awareness exercises, 46-57
collage of role of researcher, 49
constructing a yaya box, 50, 51f, 52f
describing photograph, 55-56
haiku on role of researcher, 54-55, 57f
journal dialogue, 53-54, 78-79, 80-81
with photography, 48
writing one's name, 46-48, 47f
Self-evaluation, 17f, 18f, 26f, 82
Spradley, J. P., *The Ethnographic Interview*, 30
Subjectivity, 61-62
Successful Focus Groups (Morgan), 39
Summative evaluation, 18f, 27, 83
Symbolic interactionism, 5-6

Theoretical frames, 5-7
Theoretical postures, 5
Thucydides, 61
Triangulation of data, 119

Van Manen, Max, 6

Wolcott, H. F., *The Art of Fieldwork*, 59

About the Author ■

Valerie J. Janesick (Ph.D. Michigan State University) is Professor of Educational Leadership and Policy Studies (ELPS), Florida International University, in Miami and Fort Lauderdale, Florida. She teaches classes in qualitative research methods, curriculum theory, curriculum planning and evaluation, and developing intercultural awareness in education. She has taught qualitative research methods at SUNY Albany, Gallaudet University, and the University of Kansas. Her work in international curriculum development and on international perspectives and cultural use of languages in the educational setting has enabled her to travel widely. Her writings have been published in *Curriculum Inquiry, Anthropology and Education Quarterly*, and various education journals. Her chapter in the Denzin and Lincoln *Handbook of Qualitative Research* is "The Dance of Qualitative Research Design." She is looking forward to her next projects on ethics and the qualitative researcher and taking classes in Irish step dancing.